Praise for *The Paper Solution*

"Systems are the engine to create efficiency in the home. *The Paper Solution* gives practical tips and tools that allow us all to free up our precious time to focus on what truly matters."

—Eve Rodsky, *New York Times*–bestselling author of *Fair Play*

"Drowning in paper? With Lisa's ingenious methods, you can take control, get more organized, and free up incredible amounts of time. You'll never lose a day to hunting down a permission slip again."

—Laura Vanderkam, author of *Off the Clock* and *168 Hours*

"Professional organizer Lisa Woodruff brings a fresh and realistic approach to paper. I loved that she didn't tell me to get rid of everything. Lisa shares a method for handling paper in a way that eliminates the unnecessary and keeps what's needed right where you'll easily find it. A must-read for anyone who has ever struggled with too much paper and wondered if they are keeping and shredding the right documents. Read this and you'll know what to do with everything that comes your way."

—Becky Rapinchuk, author of *Clean Mama's Guide to a Healthy Home* and *Simply Clean*

"*The Paper Solution* walks you step by step to conquering the paper dilemma in your home.... Her tips are practical and doable, leaving readers feeling empowered!"

—Maria Dismondy, author, speaker, and publisher of Cardinal Rule Press

"Lisa's enthusiasm for productivity and organization shines through every chapter of this book. Her easy-to-follow implementation strategy makes quick work of overwhelming paper piles, and the comprehensive detail within each chapter assures all paper clutter questions have an answer. Lisa is the expert on all things 'paper clutter,' and *The Paper Solution* is proof! This go-to resource provides the information, structure, tools, and motivation to properly manage your paper clutter and stop it from taking over your home and life."

—Andrea Dekker, professional organizer and blogger at AndreaDekker.com

"Even in our digital age, paper remains one of the biggest sources of clutter both at home and in the workplace.... In *The Paper Solution*, Lisa Woodruff has presented a practical, actionable approach to solving that problem. I found myself tabbing pages and highlighting sections that spell out easy-to-follow steps for clearing our homes and workspaces of paper clutter. I can't wait to share this encouraging and truly helpful book with my friends, colleagues, and listeners."

—Laura McClellan, lawyer, productivity coach,
and host of *The Productive Woman* podcast

"It's a miracle! A system of managing papers (and my life) that works in tandem with my ADHD brain (and those of my clients). The Sunday Basket concept is so simple, yet so brilliant. The book takes you through the entire system, step by step. Great reference and great program. Highly recommended!"

—Linda Roggli, award-winning author and founder of the ADDiva Network

the paper solution

WHAT TO SHRED, WHAT TO SAVE,

and HOW TO STOP

IT FROM TAKING OVER YOUR LIFE

LISA K. WOODRUFF

with Mary Nolan-Pleckham

G. P. Putnam's Sons | New York

AUTHOR'S NOTE

The stories in *The Paper Solution* are all true, and they're gleaned from my personal experiences, the stories of clients I've worked with, and anecdotes that podcast listeners and Organize 365 community members have shared with me. Some of the identifying characteristics have been changed in certain stories, and a few stories have been combined in the editing process. But it's important to me that you know that you're not alone in dealing with the paper tsunami in your life—this is an issue in homes and with families everywhere. And the good news: there's a solution. Read on. . . .

PUTNAM
— EST. 1838 —

G. P. PUTNAM'S SONS
Publishers Since 1838
An imprint of Penguin Random House LLC
penguinrandomhouse.com

Copyright © 2020 by Lisa Woodruff

Penguin supports copyright. Copyright fuels creativity, encourages diverse voices, promotes free speech, and creates a vibrant culture. Thank you for buying an authorized edition of this book and for complying with copyright laws by not reproducing, scanning, or distributing any part of it in any form without permission. You are supporting writers and allowing Penguin to continue to publish books for every reader.

Library of Congress Cataloging-in-Publication Data

Names: Woodruff, Lisa K., author. | Nolan-Pleckham, Mary, author.
Title: The paper solution: what to shred, what to save, and how to stop it from taking over your life / Lisa K. Woodruff, with Mary Nolan-Pleckham.
Description: New York: G.P. Putnam's Sons, 2020. | Includes index. |
Identifiers: LCCN 2020016464 (print) | LCCN 2020016465 (ebook) |
ISBN 9780593187760 (hardback) | ISBN 9780593187777 (ebook)
Subjects: LCSH: Orderliness. | Records—Management. |
Personal archives—Management. | Time management.
Classification: LCC BJ1533.O73 W673 2020 (print) | LCC BJ1533.O73 (ebook) |
DDC 651.5/1—dc23
LC record available at https://lccn.loc.gov/2020016464
LC ebook record available at https://lccn.loc.gov/2020016465

Printed in the United States of America
10 9 8 7 6 5 4 3 2 1

Book design by Lorie Pagnozzi
Charts by Shannon Plunkett

TO MY HUSBAND, GREG,
AND OUR CHILDREN,
JOEY AND ABBY. YOU MAKE OUR
HOUSE A HOME.

CONTENTS

PART I

we are drowning in paper

Chapter 1

The Paper Tsunami: *Why Paper Is So Important—and How to Keep Much, Much Less of It* 3

Chapter 2

The Hidden Cost of Paper: *Why It's So Hard to Let Go—and What It's Really Costing Us* 13

Chapter 3

How *Not* to Organize Paper: *What Marie Kondo (and Your Grandmother) Got Wrong* 30

PART II

how do i get started?

Chapter 4

The Paper Solution Program: *A New Way to Think About the Paper in Your Life* 45

Chapter 5

The Big Purge: *What to Shred, What to Save, and How to Tell the Difference* 59

Chapter 6

The Sunday Basket: *Where to Put Your Most Important Paper* 81

Chapter 7

Customize Your Sunday Basket: *How to Modify the Sunday Basket for Your Life* 112

Chapter 8

Create Your Calendar: *How to Get from To-Do to Done* 145

PART III
ditch the filing cabinet

Chapter 9

The Binder Solution: *Why the Best Storage Is Portable* 163

Chapter 10

Your Household Reference Binder: *How to Organize the Papers for Your Physical Home* 178

Chapter 11

Your Financial Organizing Binder: *How to Organize Past, Present, and Future Monies* 191

Chapter 12

Your Medical Organizing Binder: *How to Organize Your Medical History and Diagnoses* 201

Chapter 13

Your Household Operations Binder: *How to Organize Your Family's Fun and Daily Living* 212

Chapter 14

Your School Memory Binder: *How to Organize Childhood and School Memories* 222

Chapter 15

Your IEP Binder: *How to Organize Your Child's
School and Medical Records* 230

PART IV

how to archive the rest

Chapter 16

The (Right) Way to Archive Papers: *Where to
Store the Stuff You Just Can't Part With* 241

Chapter 17

Maintaining Your Systems: *How to Stay Organized Even
When Life Happens* 247

Chapter 18

Going Digital(ish): *When to Scan and How to Integrate Digital
Solutions to Paper Organization* 257

Conclusion 273
Acknowledgments 275
Appendix 279
Notes 293
Index 297

the
paper solution

Part I

we are
drowning
in paper

CHAPTER 1

The Paper Tsunami

Why Paper Is So Important—and How to Keep Much, Much Less of It

A paper tsunami is coming, and we need to be ready. Some of us have already experienced it, and many more will soon face the deluge. Our houses are full of paper, our parents' houses are full of paper, and some of us have *grandparents'* houses full of paper, too. That's generations of clutter waiting to crash down on our unsuspecting heads!

But there's a better way. You can ditch the filing cabinets stuffed full of documents (that you may or may not ever need to look at again). You can find the papers you *do* need easily, effortlessly, and without stress or drama. You can create a system for organizing your paper that actually works *for* you, not against you.

I know, because I was once where you are sitting right now—staring down a paper tsunami, filled with dread and uncertainty—and I've come out the other side.

Why I Care So Much About Paper

My name is Lisa Woodruff. Yes, I am one of those crazy-productive, ultra-organized people you love to hate. Yep, I was born that way. My closets were always neatly organized, and I live for a finished to-do list. (Sorry.) But even *I* found myself completely flummoxed and overwhelmed when it came to dealing with one particular type of clutter: paper.

My own personal paper tsunami came at one of the most chaotic times in my life. In the spring of 2009, my father, after being ill for nine months, was sent home with hospice care. He died just a few short days later.

As I made the final four-hour drive home, I kept my mind busy making lists upon lists. My sister and I would need to make funeral arrangements. The house needed to be cleaned, its contents dispersed and sold—sooner rather than later was best, since neither of us had the means to hold on to it. The to-dos involved with settling an estate were overwhelming. A quick Google search helped with all but one major question: what to do with all the paper.

My father's house contained a lifetime of paper, and each file would need to be sorted to settle the estate. Paper is tedious. The precious few days I had at my father's house were not enough to figure out what to do with each piece of paper. So I swept it all up and brought it home. Boxes and boxes of paper.

With my sister finishing the physical distribution and sale of the family home, I set to work settling the estate paperwork. I never felt as overwhelmed as when I went through my father's files. Part of me felt like I was invading his privacy, worried I would find something he didn't want me to see. Likewise, it was hard for me to simply trash some of the paperwork that was precious to him but meaningless to me, like his car catalog collections.

Oh, those car catalogs! Beautiful cars were Dad's passion, and he kept meticulous files full of bulky paperwork all about them. Cars he'd owned decades ago. Cars he wanted to own one day. That collection was his pride and joy, even though it had no monetary value or purpose.

It was also the bane of my existence.

So what happened to the bulk of Dad's papers? They sat there, in my home. Taking up physical space, yes, but more important, taking up precious mental and emotional real estate. My home was filled with my father's files and boxes of memories that I didn't know how to process or enjoy. Every day was filled with anxiety. Something had to give.

On New Year's Day 2012 (that's almost *three years* after Dad's papers landed in my house, for those of you keeping score), I made a vow to finally get all that paper in order. That included dealing with my own paper as well as my father's. Because I found very few books or resources that specifically addressed how to organize paper, I soon realized I was on my own. I took a deep breath, dug in, and for the next three months—through trial and a lot of error—I dealt with the paper, sheet by sheet. (Even those out-of-date car catalogs, which I recycled in the end.) Eventually, my home became close to being manageable again.

I'd turned my paper problem into the Paper Solution.

I started blogging about my experience, with the goal of sharing advice with others facing the same sort of paper crisis.

And people really responded! Some of them were, like me, cleaning out a family house or a loved one's estate. Others were simply overwhelmed by the school forms, monthly bills, medical forms, and other detritus of everyday life. My blog, Organize 365, spawned a newsletter that attracted tens of thousands of devoted fans, then a hit podcast, and, eventually, a thriving business.

Here's what I realized: although people interested in decluttering can find plenty of videos, books, and other resources about how to get rid of extra clothes, housewares, and "junk," *no one was talking specifically about how to organize paper.* And yet paper is one of the most common—and anxiety-producing—kinds of clutter that most of us have to deal with. Why is that?

What *Is* It About Paper?

Paper is the bane of most people's existence—even the most organized person will break out in a cold sweat at the thought of sorting a mountain of paperwork. So why is it so hard for even otherwise tidy people to get their heads around their paperwork?

For starters, it's the sheer volume of paper we're all faced with on a daily basis. When personal computers were first developed, we were promised they would lead to a society with less paper; but forty-plus years later, we are still not there. Although the "paperless office" was first proposed in a *Businessweek* article way back in 1975, today the average office worker is still estimated to come in contact with about ten thousand pieces of paper every year.[1]

And we're not just overwhelmed with paper at work. Americans face a daily deluge of paper at home, too—it comes in the mail, kids bring it home from school, our activities send out newsletters and calendars—and we often get behind in its management. The average American household processes a paper stack as high as a two-story house every year![2]

And the paper keeps coming! The United States Postal Service delivers over 484 million (million!) pieces of mail each day.[3] The majority of the 4 million tons of junk mail that Americans receive annually ends up in landfills.[4] This does not even begin to include the heavy amount of paper that we actually want or *need* to keep.

Paper is not pretty. It is not fun. It *is* practical, but it can also be tedious and nerve-racking. Paper piles are easily hidden—at first. For a long time, I debated with myself about how long I should save different papers, where to file papers I wanted to be able to retrieve, and why I couldn't find a particular paper. It was a waste of time—and it was stressful. And that stress builds up over time—until those piles just can't be ignored.

Although we desperately long for the paperless future, we are not there. No matter how electronic our lives become, we will always be dealing with paper. This growing volume of paper doesn't feel like a resource or a blessing—it feels like a burden.

So what do we do about it?

It is time to take control of paper instead of being controlled by it. We have to make decisions about these papers, find places to store them, complete some of them, and retrieve them when we need them. If we do not control our paper, it controls us.

So I Should Buy a Filing Cabinet, Right?

No! Dealing with your paper tsunami does not mean buying a filing cabinet. The average filing cabinet holds eighteen thousand sheets of paper, and "filing" your papers is often a way to avoid dealing with them head-on. Before you can buy an organizational product, you need to first create an effective paper management system.

Even though some of this paper is actually useful, it's no good to any of us if we can't separate the "good" paper from the "bad" paper. It's estimated that the average American will lose an average of 2.5 days per year looking for things.[5] I've found that even a well-organized filing cabinet (filled with perfectly filed papers you don't need) leads to more lost papers—and more stress—than it's worth.

Even worse, many Americans spend an average of $90 *each month* on a storage unit outside the home.[6] Listen: storage units are great for short-term storage or specific life events, but if we are paying to store stuff (including paper) month after month, only to never look at it again, we are wasting our money, time, and energy. When I have assisted clients in organizing their paper, generally 85 percent could be recycled or shredded. However, it takes time and energy to sort the active and reference papers from the piles that accumulate all over the house. How do you know which 85 percent to get rid of and which 15 percent to keep?

As a professional paper organizer, I find that the number one daily organizational challenge for people is getting (and keeping) a handle on their paper. A glance at a typical kitchen counter reveals piles of coupons, bills, school notes, directories, calendars, photos, mail, catalogs, and more. Almost every person I have heard from in my business believes that if you file it, you will forget it. This is paralyzing.

But I'm here to tell you: it doesn't have to be like this.

Paper organization is a skill. And it can be taught.

Why I Still Love Paper

So after reading this book, you probably think that I'm an avowed anti-paper crusader, determined to browbeat you into discarding all your precious paper and bring you kicking and screaming into an all-digital world. But you'd be wrong! I actually adore paper.

What?! Why?

Paper is easy. It's tangible. It's portable. As a professional organizer, I can much more easily teach you how to organize physical paper versus virtual files. And the truth is, paper is not going anywhere. So we have to figure out how to deal with it effectively.

But before you can organize the paper you need, you must first understand why paper is taking over our lives. That's what I'll explore in Part I of this book: how we got here, and why your current paper solutions probably aren't working.

Then, you need to get rid of the 85 percent of your household paper you don't actually need. That's where Part II of this book comes in: how to do the Big Purge and get rid of a big chunk of the paper that's weighing you down. You'll also learn the tenets of the Sunday Basket method, which I've used to streamline the weekly paperwork needs of thousands of clients.

So once you can actually see the paper you need, how do you manage it more effectively? That's where Part III of this book comes into play. I'll teach you about the binder method I've developed after working with thousands of people: keeping the bulk of my necessary physical paper organized in a few key binders that allow me to direct my family, even when I am not home, to retrieve the paper in question in my absence.

And for those few but important papers that you have to hang on to for the long haul—birth certificates, Social Security cards, passports, insurance paperwork, and the like—I'll teach you an archival method in Part IV. I'll also show you how to maintain these systems (even when life gets messy) and when, yes, digitization can help in certain situations, too.

The Promise of *The Paper Solution*

This book will be your guide to getting your papers organized to be useful, productive, and profitable.

Imagine the life that awaits you. Being able to put your hands on a physical piece of paper will add speed to your transactions, add weight to your verbal arguments, improve your memory, and give you confidence in your home organization.

I know this sounds like a pipe dream to some of you right now. I promise it's not. You may not be "naturally organized," but you can learn to create a system to organize your papers, a system that's customized to you and that works for your family.

In the end, I spent a whole year getting my home and paper

in order. I then spent the next six years building systems that work and learning how to teach others to apply these same systems and skills. And today (after that somewhat rocky start), I can admit it: I now *love* to sort paper! But that came only after I developed the system that's at the heart of *The Paper Solution*.

Through my own journey, I realized there's a real hunger for this information out there—for someone who provides real answers, not just a blanket statement to throw away all your books or trash all your photos.

As I share with you the tools you'll need to learn to get and keep your paper organized, I will also include some lessons about how *where* you are in life affects *how* you make decisions—and how you deal with paper. One of the most important things I have learned is that paper organizing needs to be personalized and adapted to your life stage and phase. The way we handle paper is greatly influenced by our generation. The paper organization we learned growing up, at work, and in our personal life greatly influences our comfort with making decisions about paper and how we store and retrieve it. This book will help you to understand your own stage of life and generational influences on paper management.

Life is full of unexpected events. There are celebrations like weddings, new babies, and new jobs. There are losses, illnesses, divorces, and deaths. Each life change we face comes with new incoming papers, and we need a method and a system that flexes with these events. *The Paper Solution* has been developed to do that as well.

Your own paper tsunami is coming (or maybe it's already here)—that's why you've picked up this book. My goal in these pages is to give you a system to help you get your paper organized so you can be prepared to help your friends and family do the same. Paper organization requires an investment to be successful, but it is an investment in yourself. When you make paper organization your new priority, you will start to see a reduction in all the other costs associated with disorganization and clutter.

Today, I live and breathe paper. My organizing podcast has more than seven million downloads, I teach a masterclass on paper organizing to thousands each year, and I even created my own products to help you replicate my results in your own home. But I know from firsthand experience how tricky it can be to get your paperwork in order—and to devise a plan to keep it tidy and organized moving forward. I want to share my journey and my hard-won paper knowledge with you, so you can have an easier time taming your paper tsunami than I did with mine.

I will show you how I think about paper and where it all goes. I will show you how to be more productive, more proactive, and how to plan. I am with you every step of the journey: to encourage and motivate you, to share stories, and to help you reach your goals. You will take back your home and have time to live the life that you are supposed to live.

I decided a while ago the need for paper was not going away. I could either complain and be frustrated or change my attitude. I chose the latter. I have come to love paper. I hope you will, too!

CHAPTER 2

The Hidden Cost of Paper

Why It's So Hard to Let Go—and What It's Really Costing Us

FACT: 45 percent of women polled listed piles of paper as one of their top three types of home clutter.

("Napo Statistics," National Association of Productivity & Organizing Professionals, https://bit.ly/2OmLfGW)

For seven years, 50 percent of my family's take-home pay was used to pay medical bills.

That's difficult enough, but the stress of dealing with a sick family member was compounded by the never-ending stream of bills, letters, papers, and notices from various insurance providers and doctors' offices. If you've ever dealt with a medical issue in your own family, I'll bet this sounds familiar. The stress of caring for your kids, earning enough to cover your expenses, and maintaining a semblance of a happy home life is excruciating. It almost broke me. Many days I would chant to myself, "You can make it one more minute. You can make it one more minute." Just thinking about those years raises my anxiety level.

I was so angry. And desperate. Desperate for solutions, money, resources, and sleep. There was never enough of any of it. I would wake up in a cold sweat at least once a week remembering an important item on my to-do list that had been left undone or a bill that needed to be paid.

Things came to a head one Monday morning—I had a stack of what insurance companies call EOBs (Explanation of Benefits—basically, a list of what they would pay and what I owed) that I'd been shoving into a pile on my desk, too overwhelmed to focus. But that day, armed with a cup of coffee and a can-do attitude, I was determined to get a handle on what I owed. As I dug in, I realized that I was actually accruing more fees and costs every month because I wasn't staying on top of the blizzard of notices I'd been receiving. Several claims that should have been accepted had been mistakenly rejected by my insurance company. And I was perilously close to missing the deadlines to resubmit those claims for reimbursement. I didn't have a plan back then for how to organize and file the paperwork as it came in. And it was costing me—big time.

I took a deep breath, started matching up what was paid and unpaid, and began calling the insurance company and our providers to figure out what we actually owed. That week I logged over thirty hours on the phone. I spent that week sorting papers to get our claims paid, and determined what we had left to pay ourselves.

How did I get to that point? I had become so overwhelmed

by my situation that I didn't want to face it directly. I knew it was bad, but my avoidance almost cost us thousands of additional dollars in late fees and missed insurance deadlines. After six weeks of diligently working on the phone each Monday with all the relevant parties, I finally had our medical debts organized and a plan to tackle them. But I realized then just how much my clutter had been costing my family.

What Is Your Clutter Costing You?

A chaotic life isn't just frustrating—it's expensive. Clutter and disorganization can cost us financially, rob us of our time, take a toll on our physical health, impair our social interactions, and create significant opportunity costs in all aspects of our lives. The actual costs will vary from person to person. But often the reason clients come to me is because the cost—financial or emotional—of hanging on to the excess paper in their life has become too high. They need to find a new way forward.

We all think we know what clutter is, but do we really recognize it—especially the paper clutter? Part of the reason paper piles up is that it seems so essential. Many of us actually feel safer with extras or duplicates around us. We've been conditioned to "shop big" at Costco, to hang on to those old *National Geographic* magazines to read "someday," to keep old bills "just in case" they come in handy in the future. Part of being able to get rid of our paper clutter is being able to identify the clutter in the first place.

We'll talk soon about how to sort out the 85 percent of paper that's clutter to find the 15 percent that's essential. But first, we need to really understand the price of the paper you're hanging on to. More paper doesn't always give you more safety or security or value. I'm here to tell you: you will actually feel more freedom with *less.*

When you have fewer papers, you have less to clean up. Less to file. Less to shred. Less to keep track of. Despite all these perks of less, it is hard to get rid of the excess. We worry that we may need that paper one day, to prove *something* to *someone.* (Just who and what that something and someone is, we're not quite sure.)

Most of the worries live only in our imaginations. Almost every piece of paper on the planet (except a few special memories) can be replaced with either time or money if we really need it. Honestly, you can even get a new car title, birth certificate, or passport if you must. How easy would it be to get another copy of that recipe you already found on the internet? Not hard at all. The more paper you keep, the more complicated your life and home become. The more complicated it is to process, file, manage, and purge your papers. What are you gaining from all this chaos? I would argue, nothing. It is *costing* you!

What if decluttering and organizing your paper gave you *more?* You would actually have more time, more money, more freedom, and more peace. Paper clutter has a cost every day for every person who has not created a system to manage the deluge of incoming and active papers. Study after study shows that people (especially Americans) face several different kinds of costs that arise from clutter and poor paper management. First, we will take a look at the cost of clutter and disorganization in our lives. Let's examine several different types of costs associated with living a disorganized and chaotic lifestyle.

As you consider how you want to live your life, think about what your paper clutter is costing you—and what you stand to gain from letting it go. You will regain the time you spend searching for important documents every time they're needed. You will recapture the sense of well-being that comes from knowing that your house is in order. You will have more energy and focus to give to those you love. And best of all, you will make space in your life to live the purpose that is your unique reason to exist.

Financial Costs

One of the most obvious costs of disorganized paper is, of course, financial. Have you ever headed out to a store to return an item but ended up keeping the item because you could not find the receipt? What about the coupon you know you had just the other day but cannot find, resulting in paying full price for an item you now need? Or the refund check from several years ago you found in a pile of old bills . . . but now the bank won't accept it?

"I can't tell you how many times I've kept an 'inexpensive' item of clothing rather than returning it to the store because I've misplaced the receipt," said Marjorie, a client I worked with who started adding up the costs of all those "cheap" shopping misfires. "As a result, I have dozens of items that probably still have the tags on them in the back of my closet adding up to hundreds of wasted dollars—and even more clutter to contend with!"

The costs continue to pile up. We end up paying late fees on bills we did not pay on time, even when we had enough money in the bank. Between 25 and 33 percent of Americans are late paying their bills.[1] US credit card companies collected $12 billion in late-payment penalty fees alone in 2016.[2] And research shows that about 23 percent of people pay late, not because they don't have the cash but because they can't find the bill![3] We may also acquire bank fees for overdrafting when money leaves our account because we forgot about a scheduled payment. Other times we find that we owe tax penalties because we lost our substantiating documentation for a deduction. In the worst case, late payments can lead to utility services being shut off, and an extra reconnection fee adds even more financial costs to the disorganization penalty.

We also accrue a cost for the things we purchase but never use, because we do not have a way to keep track of the associated paper. Lost or misplaced checks, cash, gift cards, and return receipts are all-too-common ways we lose money to clutter or disorganization. In 2014 alone, $1 billion in gift cards went unclaimed, and at least some of those were lost or forgotten.[4] Purchases of books, learning programs, or meal-planning courses that go unused are just wasted money.

Missing or lost vital paperwork also has a very real financial cost. When we misplace our birth certificate or a title to a vehicle, there is a fee to obtain a replacement. It is even more expensive when we need the document quickly and pay a higher price for expedited processing.

Before we started working together, Jackie was one of those clients. Her family was preparing for their first cruise when she realized her passport would expire while they were gone. And whoops!—one of her children's passports was already expired.

(You did remember that kids' passports last for only five years, not ten, right?) Jackie had to take more time off work to get the application processed, *and* pay an expediting fee. But the worst part of the whole experience was waiting for the passports to come in the mail. Until she had them in hand, she couldn't relax.

Missed appointments and cancellation fees may be more related to disorganization in life and scheduling, but these can also be caused by paper disorganization. Missing early-bird deadlines for enrollment in kids' programs has an extra financial cost. Disorganization can lead to late booking for vacations and travel, and that comes with a premium price tag.

And as we discussed before, storage fees for clutter are a huge financial cost, especially for Americans. It is estimated that one in ten Americans is currently renting storage space outside the home.[5] And most of the storage space customers *already* have a home with a typical storage space like a garage, attic, or basement. The average cost of a storage unit is $90 per month.[6] This does not include the time spent to move items in and out of the units, or the gas for the vehicles to shuttle the items back and forth to the storage units. While it is a useful tool for short-term storage for life transitions like moving, long-term storage creates an ongoing bill when the owners of the items fail to go back and remove their belongings.

You work hard for your money, and spending it on clutter and disorganization is a disheartening waste of a precious resource. We'll learn how getting a handle on your paper can lead to significant monetary savings over time.

Physical Costs

When our paper (and other clutter) is out of control, it can create chaos in our homes: what I call the physical costs of mess. Even if we don't spend money on off-site storage, the physical costs of moving, hiding, and finding paper in a cluttered home are significant.

If you are a person who gathers up and stashes paper in a closet or under the bed when guests are coming over, think about how hard it is to use those spaces for their intended purposes. When you cannot keep your clothing in your closet because it is full of boxes of paper, then you have to store the clothes somewhere else. And the items that *should* be stored where the clothes are (instead of in the closet) are also displaced—it's a clutter-strewn domino effect. Moving things around the house to stash them like this also has a time cost and frequently has a financial cost, when people forget to pull their paper back out and take care of it.

Michelle was a "serial paper pile shifter." She lamented, "I always struggle to keep track of the copious amounts of paper my daughter's school sends home. Between homework, announcements, and permission forms, I'm getting a dozen or more sheets of paper each week." It didn't make sense to file away this kind of transitory paper, but she didn't want to throw it away immediately, either—what if she forgot next weekend's PTA potluck?

"All that school paper ends up on the kitchen table—and we shuffle it around every morning before breakfast," Michelle said. "*Not* a great use of time."

Taken to its paper-strewn extreme, many people lose a

room (or even rooms) to stashes, stacks, bags, and boxes of paper that need to be dealt with. Rooms that end up being used for storage cannot be used for their intended purpose. Flat spaces like tables are often unusable. And you are paying to heat, cool, and light those rooms in your house, even if you can't access them! Most of the time, the papers in those rooms aren't even being used, so the space is both inaccessible and unnecessary.

So what's a person supposed to do? Many times they simply move—and buy an even larger home in order to hold all their stuff. (I've seen it happen time and time again.) But this never solves the issue. Larger spaces generally cost more, and the utility costs are also higher. Furthermore, larger homes require higher taxes and more furniture, insurance, and time to maintain. Other times, people will find they need to buy more storage solutions for the larger space and spend money on cube systems, shelving, cabinets, and bins to store all their stuff.

And still the paper piles up.

Depending on what part of the world you live in, you may find that clutter and disorganization can lead to damage to your home over time. You may not be able to see vermin or pests in time to prevent major structural damage. You may not be able to find the warranty to get a leaking roof fixed before the leak causes expensive damage.

Maybe you're not a hoarder (yet!), but if left unchecked, your unorganized paper can lead to significant physical costs for your home. In the pages ahead, you'll learn how to stop that loss and put a plan in place to move forward more thoughtfully.

Time Costs

Paper clutter and disorganization result in huge costs of time as well. This happens to all of us, and the price we pay can be shocking. The average American wastes fifty-five minutes per day looking for lost or misplaced items.[7] We lose time looking for papers. We lose time when we do not have clear priorities or systems. And, as we become more overwhelmed by our clutter and disorganization, we zone out by scrolling through our phones or watching TV ... and lose even more time. The cycle perpetuates itself.

As we lose time to paper clutter and disorganization, we also cost ourselves even more in additional time penalties. We have to fill out extra paperwork to return our item to the store without the receipt, or even worse, we spend all that time at the store to find out we cannot return the item at all! When we cannot find our child's birth certificate for school, we have to spend time figuring out how to get a replacement and filling out the forms to request it. Or we find that we need to spend time in line at the Department of Motor Vehicles to replace a missing car title.

The funny thing is that while you know you are losing time, you do not have any time to figure out *where* you are losing it. There is *no time*! Clutter puts us in permanent "reaction mode"—doing things on a whim and putting out fires rather than spending our time consciously and with intent. And as a result, we lose the time we could be spending doing the things we love.

Our time is precious, and we have much better ways to spend it than frantically trying to find our lost papers or finding ways to replace them. That's the promise of *The Paper Solution*: more organization and, as a result, more time.

Mental and Emotional Costs

Trying to keep track of and manage all the papers that enter our homes can be mentally draining. The more family members in the home, the more papers that need to be decluttered, organized, and managed. There are grocery lists, school papers, bills, appliance manuals, bank statements, party invitations, catalogs, junk mail, and more. Every piece of paper in a home needs to have a decision made about its purpose, function, and final place. And every paper we keep will need to have the same decision reviewed over and over as long as we keep it. Every single pile and file represents a mental and emotional price we must pay to deal with our papers.

So, each additional pile or file we create adds to our mental load. Our stuff is exhausting to think about, organize, clean, move around, and clear out. When we struggle with clutter and disorganization, we often find that we face a lot of negative self-talk. We may find that we fill our brain with thoughts like, *I am just disorganized; there is nothing I can do about it,* and *I can never find anything in this house,* or *Everyone else on the planet has it together. What is wrong with me?* Over time, these destructive thoughts become beliefs that we hold in our hearts about ourselves and can limit our willingness to continue our attempts at getting our paper under control.

Other times, we keep papers because we think we should . . . but they end up reminding us of difficult or stressful times. While it may make sense to keep that poor evaluation from work for documentation for a while, it does not make sense to keep it forever if every time you come across it you feel awful all over again. That jury duty summons from a decade ago can probably be discarded, too. It's tough to figure out what to save (and what to shred), but that's all part of the process we'll go through in this book.

Look, I get it: walking into a room and looking at a pile of papers that remind us of all the promises we made to ourselves and others can be very stressful. The guilt builds up every time we need to face the deferred decisions, and the piles serve as reminders of those we have let down.

For me it was Christmas cards. In our early married life and with young kids, I loved making over one hundred Christmas cards by hand with a cute family photo complete with a short annual recap letter for family and friends.

And then we didn't send cards for over a decade. It drove me crazy. I loved keeping in touch with friends and family, but I didn't have the time to make the cards, we didn't have the money for stamps, and I had no energy to try to compile an annual letter of "achievements." But I refused to get rid of the boxes of supplies that were cluttering up one whole corner of our spare bedroom.

This story has a happy ending, by the way. We just started sending annual cards again two years ago, in a much simpler format. We now send New Year's cards: a few photos from our annual trip to the beach, mass-produced by an online card company, with no letter, sent only to a smaller list of family members. And those bulky, fancy, card-making supplies are gone, along with my guilt and anxiety.

Piles of papers can also remind us of the other costs of clutter and the mistakes we have made in the past. We may develop the bad habit of negative self-talk or use shopping to cope with our bad feelings, and the resulting clutter further raises our emotional costs.

Our mental health and emotional wellness are impacted by our level of organization and our ability to manage our paper. Getting paper under control can result in major positive changes in our emotional health.

Health Costs

The costs of clutter—specifically paper clutter—aren't just financial, physical, and emotional, either. Clutter can have a real impact on our health. When our papers and lives are disorganized, we are more likely to forget to renew our important prescriptions or we may struggle to find the paperwork necessary to get it covered by insurance.

There is a direct link between a home with clutter, disorganization, and unfinished projects and decreased mood—as well as increased levels of the stress hormone cortisol—in its family members. In the long run, this often correlates with depression and less satisfied marriages.[8] It's not a stretch to say that an organized home is one key to a happier relationship!

Finally, as levels of paper disorganization grow, there can be real physical health hazards in the home. Large, unmanaged piles of paper can attract vermin (mice, silverfish, etc.). Large volumes of paper clutter can also create dust, which can exacerbate respiratory issues. In the worst cases, paper can actually accumulate to levels that block safe passage through the home, leading to fire or falling hazards.

Our physical health can be either improved or worsened by the state of paper in our homes. Through this process, you'll learn how to protect your physical health (and maybe improve your marriage along the way!).

Social Costs

Being cluttered and disorganized can have a real and lasting impact on our social wellness. Having piles of paper scattered around the house means you probably won't want to have guests over as often. This leads to less social support and more isolation, especially as we age. Clutter in our homes can impede our ability to deepen our friendships. We may feel inclined to invite a friend or neighbor into our homes, but if we are overwhelmed and embarrassed by our clutter, we may hesitate to do so.

At other times, disorganization in paper can result in double-booking events or missing out on social opportunities. Sometimes it can result in a missed registration deadline. Relationships with friends and family can be strained when we are not reliable in our commitments.

Paper disorganization and clutter can also impact the social health of our children. We may find that we do not have paperwork or school forms for our kids. They may miss field trips, sports camps, or other events that their friends are participating in. We often wonder if there is judgment from other parents when we are convinced we just cannot get our life together.

Kimberly told me about the shame she felt when she'd mislaid the invitation her son had received to attend his best friend's seventh birthday party. "I felt like the worst parent on the face of the earth," she said with tears in her eyes. "I just ... misplaced it. There's so much paper coming in and out of my house each week. I don't really have a way to keep track of it all."

That's exactly what we all need: a single, unified process to keep track of the paper in and the paper out of our homes, so that important bills, notices, and, yes, invites, don't get overlooked.

Opportunity Costs

This is the biggie. Hold on to your seats. When our lives are packed with clutter, either physical or paper, we miss registrations, discounts, and other events. When our lives are too full, there is no room for new opportunities. Opportunities come in the margins in our lives. We need space on the calendar, in our physical homes, and time in the day. Open spaces invite new opportunities and items to add value to our lives, passions, and purpose.

So many times our papers represent dreams and ideas rather than useful, functional, productive, and profitable pursuits. Look around the room you are sitting in. Do you have stacks of recipes to make "someday" in your kitchen? Do you have boxes of photos to put into albums or scrapbooks? Are there magazines or catalogs you are meaning to read? How long have those things been there? When is the last time you made progress on those ideas or projects? We collect papers based on our good intentions. We see information that promises to improve our lives or provide a new opportunity. But if we are not taking actual steps toward these false "goals," we are just adding to our clutter, chaos, and life costs.

When we have too much paper, we miss out by not having enough capacity and space to allow the new opportunities into our lives. Do you have the space in your life to take advantage of new opportunities? Do you have days that are purposeful and productive? Are you in control of your life? Or are you overwhelmed and at the mercy of your papers?

A Way Forward

Even though all of us can recognize the costs of clutter, we still struggle to keep our homes from being overrun by rogue papers. Why? Even if you strive for a paperless life, you have paper. Coupons, bills, kids' artwork, school notes, alumni newsletters—and that's just what came in *today*! Where does it go?

I'll tell you where. It most often lands on your kitchen counter. You pile it there so you will not lose it. Then, when friends come over, you swoop up that pile and stash it somewhere. Even worse, you start a new pile the next day. How many piles do you have? Paper multiplies faster than rabbits!

I am going to assume that you are reading this book because you are looking for a way to finally get a handle on the paper that is overtaking your home. You're sick of spending money, time, and emotional energy staying afloat amid the paper tsunami in your life. You're ready to try a new system: one that will help you figure out what to do with the backlog of paper that's filling your home—and how to keep ahead of the deluge in the future. I have good news: you have come to the right place!

You need to take action. It is really important to understand that you are in the driver's seat and the change that you require will not just *happen* to you; it will be *caused* by you. You need to make it happen. Do not wait for someone to come rescue you, because believe me, that will not happen.

Here's my vow to you: you can learn to be organized using these tried and true systems for sorting and maintaining your paper. The Paper Solution has already worked for thousands of people. It can work for you, too. So, let's get started!

CHAPTER 3

How *Not* to Organize Paper

What Marie Kondo (and Your Grandmother) Got Wrong

FACT: If you stacked all the paper an average American uses in a year, the pile would be as tall as a two-story house.

(EarthWorks Group, *50 Simple Things Kids Can Do to Save the Earth*, Kansas City, MO: Andrews McMeel, 1990)

I'll never forget walking into this one particular consultation. One of the organizers on my team had already organized the client's clothing, but she told me she was going to need some help with the family's papers. I prepared myself for whatever was ahead.

My client, a successful working mother of six children, walked me through her beautiful, well-appointed house before taking me to the papers in question. The house was in great shape, but that wasn't surprising—my organizers had already been there. However, I knew that paper is often hiding in the stealthiest of spots in the home and that appearances can be deceiving.

And then we went in the basement.

Two thousand square feet of finished space. One large great room and two offices, beautifully renovated. The space was vast, and it wasn't messy at all. It was gorgeous! So what was the problem? It was the paper.

Oh, the paper.

Not one piece had been thrown out in seven years. Not one. But they were not disorganized, either. The client had twenty-eight filing cabinet drawers full of personal and professional papers. Over one hundred memory bins of school papers. Every spelling test, math paper, newsletter, and school notice, chronicled by grade and child. And on the floor, every square inch was covered in piles of paper, each with a classification.

Judy had saved the papers in an organized way. Every paper had meaning. But she could no longer distinguish between necessary and unnecessary papers to keep. Like so many of us, she thought if the papers were organized, they could and should be kept. When and how do you let go?

Not Your Mother's (or Grandmother's) Filing System

In chapter 1, we talked about our looming paper tsunami and why each of us will have to grapple with our own papers (or those of our loved ones) one day soon. And in chapter 2, we discussed the high cost of paper clutter. So, what's the answer? A perfectly organized filing system? As Judy realized, that's only half the answer. Because while our lives and our society have undergone a series of seismic shifts in the past century, our organizing methods (especially around paper) just haven't kept up.

One of the challenges many of us face is that we will likely be responsible for our own paper *and* the paper of loved ones. But every generation looks at organization differently, and as such, each handles their paper differently. Your filing system isn't going to look like your parents' system, or their parents' system, either. And understanding the nuances of each generation's approach is vital to being able to help our parents, grandparents, aunts, uncles, our own children—and even ourselves—manage the never-ending flow of paper in our lives.

So what are the different generations? Some of these guidelines are a little fluid, but basically it breaks down like this:

The Greatest Generation	1910–1924
Silent Generation	1925–1945
Baby Boomers	1946–1964
Generation X	1965–1980
Millennials	1981–1996
Generation Z	1997–present

As far back as the Greatest Generation, paper has been stored at home in files. These filing cabinets were set up and maintained by homeowners, who, by trade, also set up and maintained filing cabinets at their place of work. Without computers or the internet, all information was recorded and proven on a tactile piece of paper. Every piece of paper was potentially important. It was *vital* to be able to store and retrieve original documents on demand. Whether those home paper filing systems were routinely decluttered and maintained is another story (and likely varied widely). But most families had a lot of paper on hand, and much of that paper was needed and useful. However, as the pace of home life and work life increased with the booming economy and the baby boom of children underfoot, I can see how papers started accumulating.

As those Baby Boomer children (whose parents were members of the Greatest and Silent Generations) moved out, sought employment, and started families of their own, they too set up home filing systems mirroring those of their parents. But other changes were afoot as well. Desktop computers came on the scene for most Baby Boomers somewhere between ages forty and fifty-five, primarily in their work life. Those computers were mostly used at first for typing reports and creating spreadsheets—which were often printed out and filed (or piled) for some potential, possible need in the future. The amount of paper increased exponentially—and those original midcentury filing systems that Boomers grew up with weren't always adequate for the situation. But no new system took its place. And still the paper accumulated.

As Gen Xers came onto the work scene, things continued to change fast—they might not have grown up using computers much, but by the time they entered the working world, they too were using the desktop computer and—by the late 1990s— email, which was a huge disruptor for most workers. Theoretically, email led to less paper . . . unless you did what many workers did and printed out vast quantities of correspondence through newer, higher-powered, faster laser printers, which were suddenly everywhere in offices and, soon, at home.

By now, many Boomers had added a home computer for their children's education, home word-processing needs, and entertainment. And by the early 2000s, those home computers were robust enough to start to change analog consumer behavior, starting first with taking (and printing) digital photos at home. More paper.

In my observation, it was the home computers created after 2004 that really changed how we stored and retrieved our personal documents, starting with photographs. The transition from film cameras to digital cameras completely changed our trust in and expectation of digital storage. Once we could take a quality high-resolution photo on a DSLR camera that rivaled a film photo, we as a society started to move swiftly toward more digital solutions. Additionally, computer backup systems like Carbonite, external hard drives, and ultimately cloud computing gave us the security that a cloud program (like the Google Doc I am writing this manuscript on) is secure enough for me to trust that I will not lose my work as I write.

By the time the first Millennials entered adulthood in the early 2000s, they were much more comfortable with digital storage. They didn't necessarily rely on the paper backup methods that older generations had been told were necessary. And they moved more and more of their storage to the cloud. But as the Millennial generation (now twenty- and thirty-something, starting families and careers of their own) face the familiar deluge of paper that's common to everyday adult life, they find themselves uniquely unable to handle it—without the knowledge of the paper systems of their parents' and grandparents' generations.

Victoria was a perfect example. She came up to me after a workshop and whispered, "I have paper."

"Yes," I said, "we all do."

"No, you don't understand. I'm a Millennial. We aren't supposed to have paper. But we all do. And I don't know what to do with it. I can't ask my friends, because we pride ourselves on not having paper."

Mind. Blown.

Our generation, culture, geographic location, occupation, and gender all play a part in how we approach and deal with paper.

Every generation brings its own organizational mind-set—and physical baggage—into this process. But the bottom line: all these files and piles will need to be sorted through at some point. While 85 percent of what has been saved most likely can be shredded, the other 15 percent is very important. For example, those piles at your grandparents' house could have an important part of your family history or even lead to cold, hard cash. I have found both when sorting through my family paperwork! I helped a client with her paperwork when her husband died, and there were multiple six-figure investments hidden in the piles of paperwork that, thankfully, we discovered. This happens more than you can imagine.

Almost always, if circumstances lead to your having to sell your parents' home, paper is the one thing that gets boxed up to deal with *later*. Your parents' generation has likely lived in their home for decades, and therefore, there is *so* much to sort through. Paper always seems to be the thing that can be boxed up. The issue is that *later* can become decades. This can result in generations of paperwork boxed up in people's basements. After all, who has time to sort through it all?

What's Wrong with Minimalism?

OK, we know now that keeping every shred of paper like our grandparents did (even if it's beautifully organized in perfect filing cabinets) isn't the answer. So what is? Should we all become minimalists? Get rid of every scrap of paper? Live a completely unencumbered, unhampered existence? I understand why it might at first seem like a tempting solution.

Minimalism has been a growing trend and has been especially popular with the Millennial generation. Millennials are much less attached to physical objects and memories than many of the prior generations. While there is no single definition of minimalism, there is definitely a trend in social media, in home decorating, and in life decisions to "live with less."

Although minimalism has a growing following, minimalism does not provide the answer for paper clutter that is being passed down from generation to generation in growing tidal waves, adding to the coming paper tsunami. Believers of minimalism focus on removing items from their life and generally advocate living with as little as possible. But that's just not realistic when it comes to paper. Particularly in the US, there is a certain amount of paper we are required to keep. Vital documents like birth certificates, marriage licenses, divorce decrees, and military paperwork. And while some hard-core minimalists can live with very little memorabilia, many of us *want* to keep high school yearbooks, letters from friends, and cards from our late grandparents. Furthermore, there is a never-ending stream of paper that comes into our homes each and every day. There are the (sometimes) easier-to-toss catalogs and junk mail flyers, but there are also bills to be paid, greeting cards to display, artwork from our kids' school, and the things we *want* to keep, at least for a short while, like magazines and coupons for our favorite stores. Information from schools, churches, clubs, organizations, and sports further compounds the paper problem.

Although some Americans are having luck enforcing minimalism, the reality is that no matter how little paper we have, we do need a place to store it for some amount of time. The paper-free digital revolution has not come to pass, and we need a *system* for managing our paper. While the best way to manage a lot of our paper will be to release it to the recycling and shredding bins, we do need to figure out where to store the remaining paper in our homes.

What about KonMari?

I am truly grateful that *The Life-Changing Magic of Tidying Up* has become such a popular book and sold over six million copies. Marie Kondo has brought this whole idea of organizing and decluttering to the forefront of the media, and as a country, we certainly need to declutter and get organized. Her ideas have opened up the discussion for people around the world to really take a look at the stuff that they have saved and think about the kind of life that they want to live. I will give her full credit for being someone who can launch an organizing empire and get Americans to start decluttering. My hat is off to you, Marie!

But here's what I've observed in my work with thousands of people over the past decade: *The Life-Changing Magic of Tidying Up* does not work in the long term for the majority of us. I know this is a controversial statement, but I will explain my opinion based on my experience as a teacher and professional organizer. Marie and I approach many aspects of organizing differently based on our ages and countries of origin, but here I will just address paper.

The following are the sticking points in the KonMari system that my clients come up against time and time again:

1. Marie consistently brings up the ideas of perfectionism, the perfect system, and that you can reach perfection.

While Marie has slightly softened on this after having kids of her own, I have always taught my clients that I do not think that they can reach perfection. I am highly organized, but I am still not there. I actually get bored when I get anywhere close to being super productive. I create all these alternative projects I can do to make my life a little bit more cluttered. I do not want to live a perfectly minimalistic, 100 percent efficient life. I do not even believe that anyone can actually achieve a perfect life!

2. The KonMari approach to paper organization does not work.

This is the hot topic that originally set me off when I was reading Marie's book. The first time I read it, I stopped after the one and a half pages about how to organize paper. The book basically said to just get rid of all of it. I nearly had heart failure. Seriously? Just get rid of everything?

First, we still *need* to keep paper. We have permission slips for school field trips. Many families send Christmas cards. The children in our lives share drawings and stories that are precious to us. The government requires *tons* of paper every year at tax-time. The idea of discarding everything is not at all realistic. In all my years as a professional organizer, I never advised a client to discard all their paper.

Now, admittedly, I jumped the gun a bit. So when I reread that section and then I read the book all the way through, I realized that toward the end of the book, Marie does tell you how to organize paper, at least a little bit. Marie teaches that almost all paper should be thrown away and that there are only three files that you should have. Files. Not filing systems. Files. Three envelopes or three files of paper, *total*. The first one is called the "Needs Attention Box." The second one is your most used papers. And the third one is papers to save. Then, if you need a paper, you go through the corresponding file and find the one that you need.

This advice just doesn't work for most of us. We have rooms devoted to paper. We have so much paper that I estimate organizing home paper separately from organizing the contents of a home. While I do agree that Americans keep way too much paper (that's the focus of this book, after all), I have yet to see a single adult who can contain their paper lives in three small files.

Personally, I have gotten down to what I think is a very minimalistic amount of paper. But if I took it all and put it in one location, I would have a file of tax documentation, eight binders, my Entrepreneur Box, a Sunday Basket, and one hundred photo albums. And, in the past year, I also started homeschooling my daughter, so I have added two additional Homeschool Boxes to manage our paper for that.

Marie's Needs Attention Box is what I call the Sunday Basket. (More on this in Part II.) Again, this Needs Attention idea is too vague for many Americans. It does not explain where to keep the box or how to use it to give the papers the attention they need.

3. Marie does not provide enough assistance for sorting photos and memories.

Marie's suggestion to go through your photos one by one and make decisions would take at least a year for most of the people I know. It is definitely not something you can tidy all at once and have done in a day or two. It just does not happen like that in our homes. Furthermore, most of us have a hard time deciding which photos are good to keep and which ones we can let go.

Don't believe me? What do you do with the extra school pictures of your children each year after you put one in a family frame and hand others out to friends and family members? If you are like most people, you store the rest in the school envelope and save them. Who knows? We might need them someday. And they cost good money, after all. So what if they're sitting on a shelf in your spare-room closet for the next twenty years . . . ?

The bottom line: people really love to have rules. Before I became a professional organizer, I worked for years as a scrapbooking consultant (a great job—and more related to organizing homes than one might imagine). I found that the toughest part of scrapbooking for many of my clients was just getting started. So I used to give them clear guidelines: "You can have two hundred pictures in an album." That got them going! Before the "two hundred photos" rule, my clients would just shuffle pictures from box to box without making much progress. But once I gave them a number, they would divide out the pictures into stacks of two hundred and get to work.

We love to have rules; we love to be told what to do. And as soon as we are told what to do, no matter who says it, we begin to act because we now have a plan. For so many of us, whether something "sparks joy" is subjective. That is why in this book I have included *explicit* rules and directions for organizing paper. These rules—this framework—is especially important when it comes to paper. There's so much of it, and it's so varied. How do you get your paper organized and maintain a workable system? How do you decide what to keep of the adorable paintings, drawings, stories, and spelling and math tests that your kids bring home from school every day? How and where do you store all the things you do keep? And what do you do with the things you do not want? Are you allowed to throw them away? Or do you need to shred them?

See? We need help!

So, What *Does* Work?

As I've said, I happen to love paper. But most papers will never spark joy, no matter how carefully you sort and keep them. Paper is overwhelming because it has so much meaning.

The key for sorting paper is focusing on usefulness. Ask yourself: **Is this paper still useful?** (Remember: in all my experience, only about 15 to 20 percent actually is.) You may find that you have a voice in your head that says, "See, you never needed that! I do not know why we are spending all this time sorting!" Do not let that voice win. Focus on the success you find as you rescue the actionable and important papers from your files. Celebrate the success of your work to retrain your mind and thoughts.

In this book, I will help you change your mind-set about paper. I also want to show you how to create paper storage solutions. Your paper storage solutions will be portable and can be duplicated from one person in your family to another, or from one home to another. The process is clear and specific—and the benefits are huge.

Are you ready to get started?

Part II

how do i get started?

CHAPTER 4

The Paper Solution Program

A New Way to Think About the Paper in Your Life

FACT: Americans discard four million tons of office paper every year. That's enough to build a twelve-foot-high wall of paper that stretches from New York to California.
(https://mashable.com/2014/04/22/earth-day-paper-infographic/)

As a professional organizer, I am always trying to help my clients change how they think about their stuff. Magazines are often a big clutter item. Usually, that's because you buy them or subscribe to them full of good intentions to read them . . . "someday." Someday, you'll be the sort of person who has the time to sit down with a big cup of coffee and enjoy that article. Someday, you'll read that short story. Someday, you'll try that recipe. But life intervenes, "someday" becomes "never," and soon you have a teetering stack of periodicals in your living room that is ten years out-of-date. How will you ever catch up to the backlog? You won't—but as long as they are there, hope springs eternal. So there they sit. . . .

When working with clients, my first question is always, "If you could only buy three magazines this week, which three would you pick?" When I posed this question to Jamie, who had stacks of magazines in her kitchen, her family room, and her study, I was surprised to see the color drain from her cheeks and a strange expression cross her face. I quickly realized these magazines meant more to her than I had anticipated.

So, I regrouped. "Which magazines do you sit down and read cover to cover as soon as you get them?"

She said, "All of them. I read them all cover to cover as soon as I buy them."

I was in shock—*all* these magazines were *read* already?

Interesting. Usually I have to work to get my clients to see that if the magazine clutter is stressing them out, it's OK to let it go. But I realized that I had to switch gears with Jamie. She was seeing the magazines scattered around her house not as a looming to-do item causing stress but instead as proof that she'd accomplished something—physical evidence that she'd consumed the content that she purchased.

And then it hit me. . . .

The next morning, I was thirty minutes ahead of schedule, so I stopped by Starbucks on the way to Jamie's house. I got us both a tall caramel macchiato, and I brought the drinks to her home. The sweet treat was thick and warm on that crisp fall day. We enjoyed them together, and when they were gone, I turned to Jamie.

"Wasn't that delicious?" I said. She agreed.

I continued: "And now, I'm going to throw the cup away. Even though I spent $3.55 on it . . . and even though I loved it. It is empty. I enjoyed and consumed the product. Now I can get rid of it."

I looked right at her. "Your magazines are like empty Starbucks coffee cups."

Jamie looked at me, not smiling, but not looking away, either.

So then I asked again, "Are there any of these magazines you can part with?"

Her reply was, "All of them."

She literally got rid of 95 percent of her magazines. With no pain, no guilt, no regret.

Perspective is everything.

Often the paper we are holding on to represents contentment or an experience we have already consumed. What are you holding on to that you have already "consumed"?

Paper Organization Is a Process

Let's get this straight: even I recognize that paper is not always fun to organize. There is usually *a lot* of it, for starters, and managing it is tedious and stressful. There are difficult decisions about what to keep, where to file papers, how long to keep items, and all the rest. Paper can be overwhelming. Paper mountains can sap your energy and motivation.

Furthermore, paper piles can be stashed in *so* many places. Without a system for managing paper, many people believe out of sight means out of mind. And that means we are reluctant to put things away for fear we will never see them again. But paper all over the kitchen counter (where it *is* in sight) means it becomes permanent clutter in our living spaces.

Almost all of us start out by organizing bunches of papers into piles. We want to believe that if we can work through the whole pile, we can maintain the pile in the future. I felt exactly the same when I first set out to tackle my paper tsunami. I set out to "get it all done." Sometimes I even succeeded for a day or two. And then, lo and behold, I was surrounded by slips of paper, Post-it notes, and scribbled reminders everywhere.

Time is another impediment to organizing our paper. We do not usually have long, uninterrupted blocks of time to work on projects. Often, making decisions about paper and being able to complete the necessary steps (paying bills, filling out forms) requires some degree of concentration. We try to squeeze in our action steps where and when we can, such as signing permission slips as we cook dinner and reading emails in the morning before getting out of bed. You cannot organize when you do not devote time and attention to it.

All these issues conspire to keep us from keeping our paper organized. But they don't have to.

Here's the truth: no one is born knowing where to start when it comes to organizing—especially organizing paper. As we've discussed, the sheer volume of paper in our lives is *so* overwhelming. And like most challenging projects, the first step is the hardest. When we look at all our paper and try to create systems to keep all those pages organized, we become paralyzed.

Unfortunately, I do not have a magic wand, and I cannot fix all these issues that challenge our ability to get and stay organized. Organization is not a destination. It is a journey. We are never going to be "completely organized." Every day that you do even one thing to maintain or create more organization in your life, the closer you are moving to living a more organized life. I can teach you specific, detailed steps that actually do work to get your paper organized.

The Four Steps to the Paper Solution Program

For any paper-organization project, there are four steps that must be completed. The time and effort it will take to finish each step depends on how much paper you currently have in your home and how much of it you need to keep. The first two steps make the biggest difference in getting organized, and you will progress to the third and fourth steps in time. We'll go into each of these steps in much more detail in the chapters that follow, but to get you started, here are the four steps:

- *Step 1: The Big Purge = Removing the Paper You Don't Need*
- *Step 2: The Sunday Basket Solution = Creating a System to Organize the Paper You Keep*
- *Step 3: Make Your Binders = Developing a System to Make Your Papers (and Life) More Productive*
- *Step 4: Maintenance = Archiving and Maintaining a System for Life*

Each step has its own goals and strategies for success. In the pages that follow, I will describe each step from beginning to end and give you actionable strategies to get organized. I used to see decluttering and organizing as one step, but the more I work with clients, the more I realize that they should be done in sequence, because each task has its own unique focus and objective. Decluttering always comes first.

Step 1: The Big Purge = Removing the Paper You Don't Need

Having too much stuff is a near-guarantee of disorganization. So this process starts with a massive, all-encompassing, ambitious declutter. Simply put, you'll discard anything that is clearly trash or you no longer need. The more paper you get rid of in this first decluttering (what I call the Big Purge), the easier it is to manage what remains. The more overwhelmed you are and the longer you have felt unorganized, the more you need to declutter.

The idea of living with less is weird. It feels odd to get rid of things we have saved for years. But in truth, we just save too much. Some of our paper is sentimental and reminds us of good times (wedding programs) and difficult times (term papers from twenty years ago). Other things we saved because they were part of our dream for the kind of person we wanted to be or thought we could become in the future (papers from old houses we used to own or recipes for meals we would need to go to cooking school to be skilled enough to actually make). It's hard to discard perfectly good ideas, but learning to live with less gives us real freedom. Freedom to live our current, actual lives and to make new choices when we are not burdened with our past dreams.

You can never get rid of as much as you need to because your mind will not let you. It will talk you into keeping papers "for reference" or "just in case." Each time you review your saved papers, you will be able to let go of papers that previously seemed impossible to live without. As you continue to clear out, you will get to the point where you have empty space in your filing cabinet, on your kitchen counter, or on your bookshelves. Empty spaces can feel strange at first, but you will learn to appreciate how much you benefit from having less paper, and you will enjoy your new empty spaces.

Although I believe you can get rid of 85 percent of your current paper, most people cannot do that on the first try. We love to keep our paper. It makes us feel secure and protected when in reality it gets in the way of our being able to access and use the paper we need. I have found most people can declutter 20 to 50 percent of their paper at one time. However, every page that gets decluttered represents progress, and progress is much more important than perfection.

In the next chapter, I'll go step-by-step through how to do the Big Purge—the first stab at a major decluttering of your long-stored paper.

Step 2: The Sunday Basket Solution = Creating a System to Organize the Paper You Keep

Once you're done with your first pass of decluttering, the process of organizing needs to follow quickly to bring order into your newly emptied space.

So often we think that the answer to finally getting organized is to buy the right containers. We want to buy filing cabinets, color-coded file folders, and all the fancy paper management tools. But as we've seen, filing cabinets are *not* the answer.

I'm not saying I'm immune to the lure of a gorgeous filing cabinet or a perfectly colored storage bin. I love a good bin! But

I've learned that the containers I buy can (sometimes disproportionately) influence what I keep and how I store things. I end up fitting my stuff into the containers instead of buying containers to fit the stuff. This is true even when the stuff is papers. Once you have removed the nonessential papers from your home, you will need to develop systems to organize and maintain the papers you keep. Organization is more than color-coding and coordinated labels. It is putting things where you can find them when you need them.

First, let's talk about what being organized means. For me it means:

- *I know where to find things, because everything has a place.*
- *I do not spend time looking for things.*
- *I feel put together. I feel confident in my abilities.*
- *I can have friends over and my house looks good—not perfect, but good.*
- *I don't have too little or too much.*
- *I am able to make forward progress on my goals and projects.*

The heart of this organizational system is something I call the Sunday Basket.

The Sunday Basket is a designated holding place for all your actionable to-dos, including mail, receipts, items to return, forms to fill out, bills to pay, letters to read, and notes you write to yourself. This centrally located basket eliminates the piles that get created all over your house and on the kitchen counter.

Filling the basket is only step one. The second and more critical step is to go through all the items you have put into your basket each week on the same day. I do mine on Sunday. This ninety-minute sorting, doing, and planning session keeps your to-do list at bay and helps you add up to five hours in your week. Each week!

I want to give you one caution. You will not get it 100 percent right the first time. No matter what you are organizing, your goal is to get 80 to 90 percent better. You want to get the majority of your paper into systems that deal with most of your life needs. You may still occasionally lose or misplace a paper or forget to mail a birthday card. However, the more you can build systems and habits (and we will cover this in the next step), the more you can trust your system.

When it comes to the organizing step of this process, "done" is better than "perfect." A paper-organizing system that you use is much better than an imaginary perfect system that never gets implemented. Also: the system that meets your needs today will *have* to change tomorrow. That is not failure. That is life. But in this book, I will teach you a system that can grow and flex with you no matter what phase of life you are in or what life events you are experiencing. The exact contents of your Sunday Basket and your paper files will change, but this system will allow you to adapt to whatever life brings.

Step 3: Make Your Binders = Developing a System to Make Your Papers (and Life) More Productive

When organizing paper, you will want to match the frequency that you use or reference a paper to the way you store it. **Active** papers (things to put on the calendar, bills to pay, receipts you need for errands) go into the Sunday Basket. The Sunday Basket stays open and lives on your kitchen counter or wherever else paper enters your home. Papers that you need to keep for a while and may need to **reference** get put into binders.

After analyzing hundreds of clients as I helped them organize, I concluded that 90 percent of their filing cabinets could be replaced with just the six binders in Part III of this book. And for households without children, that number was reduced to four. Just four binders.

The majority of our household paper falls into these four categories:

- **The Household Reference Binder** *encompasses all the papers for your physical house: warranties, manuals, insurance, decorating colors, how to change the water filter, and how much mulch to order each year. Basically, if you sold your house, what information would the new homeowner need to have?*
- **The Household Operations Binder** *is the holding place for everything that makes your family unique. Things you would not give a new homeowner, such as pet information, party ideas, holiday notes and ideas, travel information, car information, and community activities.*
- **The Financial Organizing Binder** *was created in hindsight after settling my father's estate. The Financial Organizing Binder houses everything needed for someone to act as financial power of attorney on your behalf or to settle your estate after you pass. This binder has been reviewed by estate lawyers and will save you thousands of dollars and untold hours when needed.*

- **The Medical Organizing Binder** *is designed to house the papers and documentation needed to advocate as a power of healthcare, guardian, or caregiver for an adult. Time after time clients share with me how having a simple binder, with medical information for an ill family member, has saved redundant tests, over billing, and so, so much time.*

If you have kids, you may want to supplement these with two additional binders: the School Memory Binder and (if your child has special educational or medical needs) the IEP Binder. More on all these later in the book.

Step 4: Maintenance = Archiving and Maintaining a System for Life

Any organizing system requires ongoing maintenance. We need to shower, wash the dishes, and do laundry regularly to keep our lives in order. Organizing paper is no different. Mail is delivered six days a week. Paper comes home with us from work, and kids bring it home from school. We get cards around the winter holidays and our birthday.

Part of what I teach in Part IV is how to develop a maintenance schedule and plan. You'll learn how to archive papers that you must keep but will rarely reference (like old tax returns), how to deal with unexpected life events (and something unplanned is *always* cropping up), and how to breach the physical/digital divide (when some items can be digitized—and when other digital items should actually be printed out for safekeeping).

Order from Chaos

In the chapters that follow, you'll learn how to sort your papers, then how to organize the documents that are left, and finally, how to create a system that will help you maintain that organization for life. For those of you who, like me, love a good diagram, the process (in its uber-simplified form) looks something like this:

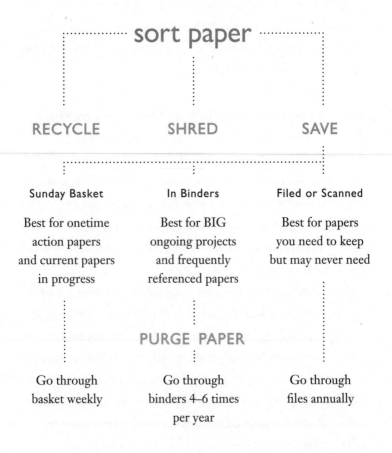

sort paper

RECYCLE	SHRED	SAVE
Sunday Basket	In Binders	Filed or Scanned
Best for onetime action papers and current papers in progress	Best for BIG ongoing projects and frequently referenced papers	Best for papers you need to keep but may never need

PURGE PAPER

| Go through basket weekly | Go through binders 4–6 times per year | Go through files annually |

The push to get organized often comes during or right after a crisis. It certainly did for me. But that doesn't mean organization needs to be perfect or precious. I believe organizing is a form of giving ourselves grace. There is no need to buy expensive products to create the best life and home you can for yourself and your family.

To get organized, you will need to do the work and think carefully about the paper you are keeping in your home. However, I promise it will be worth it.

Here are some key things I want you to keep in mind:

- Organization can be learned. *So often we grow up with the message that we are either neat or messy. Organized or disorganized. Tidy or sloppy. The reality is that organization is a life skill. There are steps anyone can take to become more organized. I want to teach you that it is OK that you were not "born organized." You certainly are not alone: 43 percent of Americans categorize themselves as disorganized.[1] I have been teaching organization skills for years, and I assure you that you have all the training you need right here in this book.*

- Organization has nothing to do with containers. *So many times I see people spend large amounts of money on beautiful, color-coordinated containers and bins to get their papers organized the way they dream of (or more often, the way they saw it on Pinterest). But soon, they are missing papers and forgetting appointments, with stacks of who-knows-what all over their homes. They return to Pinterest looking for the next planner, container, or product that will finally work. My systems do not rely on organization products. I teach you how to organize your paper and life using a process and a routine. I teach functional organizing.*

- Organization celebrates progress, not perfection. *Despite what you see on social media or when you visit your older sister, everyone struggles in this life. Our goal is to make progress. Every single step you take toward a more organized life is a step in the right direction. Celebrate the smallest wins, and keep going. "Done" is better than "perfect." Eventually, the time you used to spend under stress looking for items will convert to time you get to spend doing whatever it is you are uniquely created to do.*

- Give yourself grace. *You must take pressure off yourself. Our expectation is that you will start to take some action. You may not get through the full program right away. Life can be so incredibly hard at times. You may be dealing with a traumatic life event, a stage in life with no extra time, or a physical condition that has you down (and sometimes all three at the same time). Instead of giving yourself a hard time because you "failed" to reach your goals, take a step back and realize that it is all OK. Give yourself a break, but keep going.*

Are you ready? In the next chapter we are going to dive into the Big Purge. This will take time, but stick with it! As your paper piles start to leave, you too will feel lighter and more in control.

CHAPTER 5

The Big Purge

What to Shred, What to Save, and How to Tell the Difference

....

FACT: Each year, about 100 million households receive 16.6 billion catalogs.

FACT: The average American receives 49,060 pieces of mail in their lifetime. One-third of it is junk mail.

("Surprising Stats," *Simply Orderly,* http://simplyorderly.com/surprising
-statistics)

....

The boxes kept coming. Carload after carload of boxes, brought in on hotel luggage carts piled high. Each six-foot table was surrounded by a sea of boxes stacked three or four high. I had envisioned this event in my mind, but the reality of seeing it in person was staggering.

Years earlier, I had thought to myself, what if...

- *What if there was a way for me to help more than one client at a time?*
- *What if I could host an event with professional paper organizers on staff to answer your hardest paper-organization questions?*
- *What if we could have secure bulk on-site shredding?*
- *What if . . . you didn't have to do this alone?*

My first paper-organizing retreat confirmed my thoughts that there was a desire to go through this big paper purge with community, but I had no idea how far people would come to do so. One family of four traveled *fourteen hours* (with a van full of boxes) just to attend the weekend event with me in Cincinnati. After unloading the paper, the husband and kids explored the city while the wife sorted, purged, and organized.

Everyone was cautiously optimistic as they entered the event space that Saturday morning. Papers were sorted at a record pace for hours as the attendees tried to get through as many boxes as possible before the shredding company came at 2:00 p.m. And then as the pace slowed, the emotions began to surface.

Two of the participants brought with them piles of papers they had been stashing in boxes for years—including mail that they'd never even opened. They each felt overwhelmed and embarrassed that they had been delaying this day for so long, but once they realized that they weren't the only people living this way, their shame evaporated—and they got to work.

One woman's piles included the personal papers of her sister, for whom she had been the caregiver until her death a few years before. These were random, meaningless papers to others, but this woman couldn't part with them until she had the rules and guidance from the group to help her along the way. Tears were shed that day (and not just by her).

Two local ladies brought as much as they could that first weekend—and connected with the strategies (and each other) so much that they started getting together regularly to continue the sort on their own. They both worked full-time, had supportive yet also overworked spouses, and lamented that keeping up with their kids and houses was taking a toll. In between each paper purge, they cheered each other on to implement better productivity strategies at home and work. And they kept coming back to my weekend events—by the third retreat, they had each adjusted their work hours, increased their work productivity, streamlined their daily routines, and both felt more proactive about their parenting plans.

Nine hundred pounds of paper was shredded on-site that first retreat weekend. Another nine hundred pounds was recycled. I've gone on to lead many similar retreats with lots more participants (and literally tons of paper). But a word of warning as you embark on this first stage of the process: the Big Purge can stir up more emotions than you expect.

This part of the process is hard—I won't sugarcoat it. Even those who come to a weekend paper-organizing retreat still have more left to do. Some days will fly by and your purging will be easy. Other days a reminder of a passed pet or loved one will stop you in your tracks. It's OK. Feel those emotions, take a day off from purging, and give yourself grace. Then start again tomorrow. The Big Purge is a marathon that will prepare you later for your binder-creating sprints.

It's Time to Purge

Going through every pile and file is what we think of when we talk about getting our paper organized. The Big Purge is your step-by-step guide to touching and deciding if you want to keep each and every single paper in your house. I'm starting here because the guidelines in the Paper Solution will inform what you save (and what you toss) at every stage. **But here's a secret: you don't have to finish (or even begin) the Big Purge before you start your Sunday Basket.**

In the next few chapters, I will share with you my Sunday Basket system. This is the weekly paper-organization system I use to keep my daily mail, to-dos, and projects organized. You *can* start with the Sunday Basket system (many people do) and come back to this chapter later. You can also start the Big Purge and, before you complete it, jump over and start your Sunday Basket. Read through these chapters to see which starting point resonates with you the most. If you are unfamiliar with the Sunday Basket concept, I recommend starting with the Big Purge. If you found *The Paper Solution* after learning about and implementing a Sunday Basket, improve on that paper-organizing system first and then come back to the Big Purge. Remember that the Big Purge is a marathon. It can take you anywhere from a month to a year to accomplish this purge. Most people do it in 90 to 120 days.

Ready? This process is going to feel good. But it's also, dare I say it, a little scary and intimidating, too.

Before you dive in, a word of caution. I am not sure what particular piece of paper will trigger you, but there will be a time when you are overwhelmed in your paper organization. Regret, grief, condemnation, judgment, stress, worry, hopelessness—these are all emotions I experienced in going through my own Big Purge. We will be purging more than just paper in this chapter.

What do you do when those big emotions come? I eat chocolate and scroll Instagram. Sorry, it's the truth. It is OK to stop for the day. It is OK to save a paper you think I would purge. It is OK to call a friend and relive a memory. It is OK to cry. And have a pity party. And be mad.

It is *not* OK to give up. That is my only rule. How you process your emotions, your history, and your life is all OK, and I give you the space to do that. Just please, don't stop. Take a day, or the weekend, and then start again. It will be worth it. I promise!

Preparing to Purge

The Big Purge is a project. Your first paper project. As such, you need to prepare your project space so you have everything you need to be successful as the project progresses. This space can be in the corner of a room on a card table or at the end of the dining room table. A table space with five to six boxes, Post-it notes, a stapler, a staple remover, paper clips, highlighters, and pens will do.

I like bankers' boxes. You can get a set of ten for around $10 to $15 at any office supply store. They are an easy size to carry, with built-in handles. They are also easily stacked while you are organizing all your paper and can be moved to storage if need be.

I like to label my bankers' boxes with a thick marker so I know what paper is in each box. Here are the boxes and labels I recommend for the Big Purge:

- *To-Be-Sorted*
- *Saved Papers—these will eventually go in your Sunday Basket (active papers), your Binders (papers to be filed), and your Archives*
- *Shred*
- *Recycle*
- *Trash*

Using these labeled boxes, let me show you how your papers are going to flow through this process.

Gather Your Papers

I know you are ready to jump in and start sorting every pile you see. Remember we are in a marathon, and this box is your one-mile mark. As you work, you will grab a bunch of papers (maybe from a filing cabinet, a box in the basement, or a pile in your kitchen) and put them in the **To-Be-Sorted** box. Then, you will go through each piece and move it into one of the other boxes. Each time you fill this box and then process the contents, you've completed a mile of your marathon.

It may seem like an unnecessary step to move files from your filing cabinet into the To-Be-Sorted box, but this is the key! Removing your paper piles and files from their regular homes is the equivalent of trying on all the clothes in your closet.

For example, when you are flipping through the manuals stored in your filing cabinet, you will cherry-pick out the manuals you know you don't need. When you lug those same manuals to your paper-sorting station, you will ask yourself, "Why am I saving all these?" The physical act of taking them all out and moving them makes it just as easy to discard them than to save them. And that is what we want. To save less.

Ask: Should I Keep This?

There's only one main question to ask yourself as you do your first big sort: Should I keep this? If so, put it into the box that's marked **Saved Papers.** If not, put it into a box marked **Shred**, **Recycle**, or **Trash**.

Don't spend time organizing the papers in this **Saved Papers** box just yet. You are only determining at this stage if you want to keep a paper or not—you're decluttering, not organizing.

I know you are going to be tempted to separate various papers as you're working—perhaps to organize all your medical papers together, or all your house papers. You might skip ahead and try to sort the papers into groupings that match the categories in Part III of this book.

Don't. I'm serious. This is where you will get overwhelmed—and derailed. Trust the process. Your goal is to move *all* your paper from the **To-Be-Sorted** box into a **Saved Papers** box or out into a **Shred**, **Recycle**, or **Trash** box.

The only exception to this rule is if you come across an active paper—a bill that has to be paid next week or a party invite that you don't want to lose track of for later this month. Active papers need some short-term action: to be filled out, returned, paid, renewed, ordered, etc. Those papers you'll set aside into your **Sunday Basket** pile—and you can skip ahead to chapter 5 and start that part of the process at any time.

If You Don't Need It: Shred, Recycle, or Trash It!

Any paper you do not move to the **Saved Papers** or **Sunday Basket** box will move to one of these boxes:

- **Shred:** *This box is for any papers with sensitive information. You will want to shred anything with your birthday, Social Security number, phone number, address, and other private data.*

  1. A word of caution: you may shred as you go, but it will slow your progress considerably. I suggest completing all decluttering steps and then shredding. Don't worry about buying a paper shredder yourself, either—they are expensive and often unreliable. You're trying to get rid of clutter, not bring more of it into your home!

  2. I recommend taking your shredding to an office supply store and paying them to shred all those pages. Most office supply stores will shred up to five pounds of paper immediately. For larger amounts of paper, the employee will place your papers in a locked cage that is shredded on-site by a reputable shredding

company at regular intervals. The charge for shredding is typically by the pound, and a typical bankers' box of paper weighs twenty to twenty-five pounds. It is so much easier to pay someone else to shred the paper than it is to buy a shredder, sit down to shred, wait for the shredder to cool down from overheating, and deal with all the little scraps of paper generated.

3. Remember: anyone can shred—only you can purge!

- *Recycle: This box is for any papers that you no longer need and that do not contain sensitive or private information. Recycle as much as possible!*
- *Trash: You'll be surprised what you come across among your papers! One client of mine found a bracelet in a file folder that had been lost for at least ten years. She figured it must have slipped off her wrist and into the folder as she was working. The fact that she hadn't touched the file since was a pretty good indication that those papers could be discarded! She kept the bracelet, of course, but alongside it was a collection of old computer floppy disks—those old ones that were the size of a piece of bread and flexible. Like, from the 1980s. Even if she had the technology to read those anymore, their contents were probably the equivalent of those untouched papers in the file—out-of-date and irrelevant. Into the trash they went.*

Bottom line: give yourself permission to shred, recycle, and even trash the papers you come across. In the pages that follow, I'll give you some rules to help make that a little easier—and some ways to customize some rules of your own.

What Should You Purge?

As you work through the organizing step, look at each piece of paper and first decide if you even *need* to keep it. Think carefully about when you would actually need or use the piece of paper you are considering keeping. Get rid of as much as you can during the first sort, and you will have less to organize and manage. You will not have to spend time or energy figuring out where to save the fifth meatloaf recipe you find or which part of the binder should hold the manual for your toaster.

Our homes receive all kinds of paper every day. The fewer papers you keep, the easier it is to organize your papers today and in the future. Papers come in the mail, in our hands, and from a plethora of other sources. We get sales offers. Companies send us "opportunities" to spend our money. We get information in magazines and newspapers. We read blogs (and want to save the pages). Tons of ads appear in our junk mail every single day. We write to-do information on the backs of envelopes. We put things on the front of the fridge for "safekeeping." There are piles of scraps of paper in our purses and on the coffee table. We write ourselves reminders for today and for the future and try to keep track of them.

Some questions you can ask as you analyze each piece of paper as you sort it:

- *Did I ask for this piece of paper?*
- *Where can I find this information in the future if I want it again?*
- *How hard is it to replace this information? (Do a quick internet search and see if it comes up.)*
- *Is this information useful?*
- *How old is this information?*
- *Under what circumstances would I look for this piece of paper?*
- *Is this important for tax or legal reasons?*
- *What is the worst thing that would happen if I do not keep this?*

Every client I work with has some type of paper clutter that they have a particularly hard time parting with. I've had to convince people that, yes, you can find all kinds of quilt and knitting patterns online, often for free. Indeed, utility companies keep a year or more of bill information online for your reference. Your bank stores copies of your canceled checks. My rule of thumb: if there is something you can easily find, replace, or access using a search engine like Google, try living without the physical paper.

We only have this one life, and what is truly most important is to spend our one, precious life doing the *right* things. Getting all your paper organized will help you to have more margin in life. You will develop habits and skills to get and stay organized, and you will have more space and energy to go out and live your life purpose.

ESSENTIAL BIG-PURGE SUPPLIES
TO HAVE ON HAND

HIGHLIGHTERS

As I sort my papers, it can take me a while to figure out what the paper is and why I need it. I found it helpful to be able to highlight information as I was sorting to speed up my organizing time in Part III of this book. For example, in all my kids' educational paperwork I would highlight the report date. This also helped me see duplicate copies I would have saved. I did the same with insurance renewals we receive every six months. I would find the policy date, highlight it, and when I found another one, I would keep only the most recent policy. Now with four household drivers, I also highlight the car being insured so I just save the necessary papers for each car.

POST-IT NOTES

My mind works in overdrive. Seeing papers sparks thoughts of items I need to check, people to follow up with, and facts to confirm. Having a stack of Post-it notes allows me to add those thoughts to the papers and keep on sorting!

STAPLERS

Even if the papers I am keeping will end up unstapled in binders, I often staple the pages together as I sort so I can move quicker and papers remain together.

What Should You Save?

Good question. I researched the United States' IRS laws and came up with a list of papers you should save. Of course, you *can* save more (and always check with your own tax professional if you're unsure), but if you want to know what you *should* save, here are some guidelines.

The following documents should not be shredded:

- *Birth certificates*
- *Death certificates*
- *Passports*
- *Pension plans*
- *ID cards*
- *Marriage licenses*
- *Divorce decrees*
- *Business licenses*
- *Wills*
- *Power of attorney paperwork*
- *Military records*
- *Life insurance policies*
- *Safe-deposit box inventories*
- *House deeds*
- *Mortgage statements*
- *Annual filed tax returns*
- *Loan documentations*
- *Individual stock purchases*

Everything else is personal preference. I find it is easier to go through this process if you think about what you want to keep before you start and create a set of "rules" for what paper your household decides to keep. And that is the distinction. You can keep any and every paper you want to keep, but you need to decide that *you* want to keep it.

Let's make a few rules together so you know how they work, and then when you find yourself running across the same type of paper more than five times, make a rule and add it to the list. Here are some common rules I set up with clients as we work together:

Rule 1—Bank Statements

Q: Do you want to keep them—yes or no? If yes, for how long?

A: Yes, for three months.

Rule: If I see a bank statement that is over three months old, I shred it.

Rule 2—Insurance Statements

Q: Do you want to keep them—yes or no? If yes, for how long?

A: Only the most recent policy statement and the initial policy booklet.

Rule: When I see an insurance statement, I will keep the most recent statement and policy book.

Rule 3—Utility Bills

 Q: Do you want to keep them—yes or no? If yes, for how long?

 A: No.

Rule: All telephone, gas, electric, cable, water, trash, and recycling bills are to be shredded.

Rule 4—Coupons

 Q: Do you want to keep them—yes or no? If yes, for how long?

 A: No.

Rule: I am going to throw away all coupons and start over with new coupons.

Rule 5—Manuals

 Q: Do you want to keep them—yes or no? If yes, for how long?

 A: Keep only current.

Rule: Keep manuals for current items to be added in the binder step.*

Here are a few guidelines I share with my clients to help them establish their own rules for the unique paper in their home:

---

* In chapter 10, I will talk with you about the information you may want out of your household manuals. Most of you will recycle them after that step.

to shred
or
not to shred

A quick guide to organizing your financial and household papers

Documents Not to Shred

- Birth and death certificates
- Social Security cards
- Passports
- Pension plan documents
- ID cards
- Marriage licenses
- Divorce decrees
- Business licenses
- Wills, living wills, and powers of attorney
- Military records
- Life insurance policy
- Safe-deposit box inventory
- House deed and mortgage documents
- Annual filed tax returns

Shred When You Get the Next...

- Social Security statement
- Annual insurance policy
- Retirement plan statement
- Investment statement monthly and quarterly

Shred Once You Confirm the Transaction on Your Statement

- Bank deposit slips
- Credit card receipts
- Other receipts unless needed for warranty

Shred When Your Loan, Policy, or Warranty Ends, or You Sell the Item

- Warranty documents and receipts
- Insurance policy
- Loan documents until paid off
- Individual stock purchases

Shred After Seven Years

- Tax return preparation documentation

Shred After One Year

- Pay stubs
- Bank statements
- Credit card statements
- Medical bills—one year after payment or seven years if deducted on your taxes

Shredding Tips

Shredding is $1 a pound at most office supply stores.
A full bankers' box of shredding typically costs around $25.

STOP THE PAPER TSUNAMI
BEFORE IT STARTS

The best way to have less paper is to stop as much as you can from entering your home in the first place. Mail takes a lot of time. And most of the mail we receive is junk mail. You do not have to fix this all today, but start making a pile of paper sources you no longer wish to receive.

- For example, you can tear off the back page of catalogs you never order from. Put them in a slash pocket, and you will make time to cancel them in the future.

- You can contact organizations soliciting donations and ask to be taken off their mailing list (or be converted to email if you prefer to stay in contact).

- You can also go through the US Federal Trade Commission website to opt out of junk mail temporarily or permanently at https://www.consumer.ftc.gov /articles/0262-stopping-unsolicited-mail-phone-calls -and-email.

- You can opt out of prescreened credit card offers at https://www.optoutprescreen.com.

- The Digital Advertising Alliance allows customers to opt out of both physical mail and electronic offers at https:// www.aboutads.info/consumers.

- Consider opting in to electronic bank statements and electronic bill pay to eliminate that mail as well.

Tackling Difficult Memories

Your paper is full of memories. When I first started decluttering paper, there were many pages that reminded me of the future that I thought I would be living. They represented an unusual kind of loss, because the items were attached not to the loss of people or money. Instead, they represented a future that I thought I would have but have not experienced yet or that I know will never happen.

We all have hopes, dreams, ambitions, and pictures of our future that do not materialize in the ways we thought they would. That does not make our current reality bad. It does not make it good. But this process is a good time to look with clear eyes at the papers that symbolize those alternate realities and ask ourselves if hanging on to them serves our current life, as it is now.

Are there papers that remind you of:

- *the parent you thought you would be?*
- *the person you thought you would marry?*
- *the lifestyle you thought you would have?*
- *the career you thought you would have?*
- *the free time you thought you would have?*

These are difficult but important questions. Often, we are not holding on to things for tangible reasons. Instead we feel that if we keep them, then one day that dream or ambition may come true.

One thing that made a significant difference for me in releasing papers associated with old memories was to flip the script. Instead of focusing on what may have been, I instead focus on what I have. I never imagined that I could talk to people from my home and inspire others to change their lives based on their goals, hopes, and dreams to get organized. I am teaching and using my gifts in ways that I never imagined I would.

However, after years of working as a classroom teacher, it was extremely hard to get rid of all my teaching papers—even though they're now outdated and I have no plans to go back to that career. It took me years to let my teaching license lapse and to declutter my notes and plans. Giving up those papers was giving up a part of my old self.

Each of us has a different degree of sentimentality and is touched differently by memories. There is no right or wrong, but we want to honor our own emotions and experiences. If you tend to want to keep everything, go ahead. Fifty percent of the people I professionally organize have recently lost a loved one, and that brings a whole additional level of emotion to this decluttering process. If this is you, be kind and patient with yourself—remember: progress, not perfection. But also be aware of *why* emotions may be cropping up as you move through these documents—you're also stirring up old memories.

The last thing you want to do is give up something you are not yet ready to give up. After working with many, many clients, I've noticed that five years seems to be the magic amount of time that needs to pass before full closure settles in after a loved one's death. After that time, you can begin to process through why you saved what you saved and imagine how you could still remember your loved one without that physical possession. If you are dealing with other losses (loss of a child, loss of a sibling, loss of a friend), keep gifting yourself grace. Grief is complicated, variable, and unpredictable. Enjoy the memories in your papers whenever you can, and keep whatever feels right.

Here are five tips I gave myself that I share with clients about how to deal with papers related to memories.

1. Go through one box, file, or pile at a time.

2. If there are other family members who may want the items you are ready to part with, reach out and see if they are interested in receiving them.

3. Set a time limit for getting rid of the items you are releasing. Get them out of the house. Once things leave the house, they are no longer yours. Do not judge others if they keep or give away the items you eliminate.

4. If there are one or two things you love and want to keep, consider putting them on display where you can enjoy them. If you want to keep things tucked away, put them in a container for safe storage with a good label.

5. If there are things you want to share with others, consider taking pictures and creating heritage photo albums you can share with family or keep for your own memories.

After the (First) Purge

Overall your paper should be reduced by at least half after you complete your first sort, but ideally you will choose to keep only about 15 percent of your paper. Be ruthless. If there is information you can look up online, get rid of the paper. If the paper is about something you want to do "someday," get rid of it. The good ideas will come back. A few years ago, I decided to be so ruthless that every recipe, article to read, or decoration idea I was not committed enough to actually start within twenty-four hours was discarded. There are so many papers and ideas that come to us every single day that we cannot possibly try them all. It is fine to use online idea repositories like Pinterest to hold new ideas, but do not keep the paper piles in your home. Stick to the things you are inspired enough by to start *now*, and let the rest go. If the recipe is really that amazing, someone else will serve it at a party and you will have a chance to try it later.

Take a few minutes and put all the recycling into the correct bin and get it ready to leave the house. If you have filled your house container, take the paper to your outdoor recycling can. Figure out which day you can take the shredding to its final destination, and get it ready to go out of the house.

Congratulations! Along the way, I promise—you'll be purging even more of that paper that right now seems so essential. But next up, we're going to move to what I believe to be the core of the Paper Solution program: the Sunday Basket.

CHAPTER 6

The Sunday Basket

Where to Put Your Most Important Paper

FACT: Using the correct organizational tools can improve time management by 38 percent.

(BusinessWire, "Improved Sense of Well-Being," https://www.businesswire .com/news/home/20080103005018/en/Brother-Announces-Numerous -Studies-Link-Organization-Improved)

Once you get through at least a partial purge of the documents that are weighing you down, you'll start to feel lighter and more in control. But this doesn't address the big problem that brings so many of us to the breaking point when it comes to paper: handling the daily, weekly, and monthly papers, bills, announcements, coupons, and other time-sensitive documents—what I call active papers. That's what Joseph told me was his big issue.

"Truthfully, I could access most of our important documents even before I started the Big Purge, but I wasn't satisfied with my day-to-day paper handling," he explained. "I had files that were successful, but only when I remembered to file them! I had folders, and trays full of papers, and the kitchen island was the landing place for unopened mail and random papers. If guests were coming, I simply swept papers into laundry baskets and moved them into the spare room. And I lost track of more than a few monthly gas bills and school notices. The whole situation gave me hives!"

But when we started talking about the Sunday Basket, something clicked with Joseph. "Now I had a place to put everything! Anything that needs attention is in that basket. All papers and items are visible, and also, I physically handle them each week, which meets my needs visually and tactilely. I address each item, and it gets calendared, signed, paid, slash-pocketed, or put back. I feel like I am getting back my house, and now I have more time to accomplish *my* projects and goals."

What Is a Sunday Basket?

Now that you've tackled your first Big Purge (or even if you've just started that process), you're probably feeling pretty good. Those electric bills from seven years ago and junior year English papers from, well, much longer ago than *that* are in the process of being shredded, recycled, and removed from your house.

But now what?

Not every paper in your life can be purged.

But not every paper that remains needs to be filed.

Some papers in your life are just papers. These are the bills that need to be paid next week. The invitation to the party next month. The papers for the school PTA fund-raiser later this semester. You need them for a brief while, and then they leave your home. They will actually be out of your home *before* you could file them—and you wouldn't even want to file them, because soon they'd just be more clutter. Exactly what we've been trying to get rid of.

I know what you are thinking. Many of us have heard over and over to touch a paper only one time. So, if these are not file-able papers, then you should just do the task and trash the paper, right? Wrong.

First, you never have enough time to take action on every paper you touch. Second, every paper that needs action is not equally important. This is evidenced by the fact that you still have paper piles in your home. Even if you diligently keep any potentially important paper, if you cannot find the papers you need when you need them, there is no reason to have kept them. So, what is the solution?

You need a Sunday Basket.

The Sunday Basket is the *one* place for active, current papers in your home. The Sunday Basket is where your most important, active, time-sensitive papers are managed. Purging the inactive and redundant papers from your life was a great first start. Next, you'll use the Sunday Basket approach to get your current, active papers organized. This frees up your mind to make better decisions about what to archive and save in other categories—so you can figure out what you actually need to hang on to (in those binders that we'll cover next) and how to organize it more efficiently. As the chapters continue, more decisions need to be made, but you will have fewer unorganized papers left to deal with.

I recommend you keep your Sunday Basket in the kitchen. Even more shocking, I recommend keeping it open on your kitchen counter! It seems as though it would be adding to the clutter problem, but let's be realistic. In the typical family home, files are in the basement, and piles of paper are in the bedrooms, family room, and kitchen. Few homes actually have a home office where the paperwork is done. Even people who work from home go through their mail, bills, and kids' papers in the kitchen. So why are we fighting that? Once I embraced that the kitchen really was paperwork ground zero, I was able to create systems that actually worked to house my paper.

WHAT ARE YOUR "ACTIVE PAPERS"?

Your active papers are the papers that are everywhere all over the house. It is your to-do list, the mail, bills, the paper that comes home from the kids' school, the bulletin from church, the flyer that got left on your front door, receipts, and all that paperwork that seems to be *everywhere*. A piece of active paper is useful when it reminds us to take action on something. It might be a reminder to pay a bill online, send a snack to school, change the furnace air filter, give a pet monthly heartworm medicine, or tickets to a sports event you plan to attend. These papers need a home and a system for ensuring your reminders turn into completed actions. A Sunday Basket is the system to get this accomplished.

How Does the Sunday Basket Work?

The Sunday Basket takes about six weeks to get firmly established as a habit for yourself and your family. Let's travel forward six weeks from now and see what a fully functioning Sunday Basket looks like.

After arriving home on Tuesday at 5:00 p.m., you walk to the mailbox, retrieve the mail, and flip through the pile to see if there is something interesting. No handwritten notes or checks jump out at you, so you dump all the mail—including the junk mail—right in the Sunday Basket. Some days you recycle catalogs and sales flyers, especially if they are bulky, but for the most part, *all* the mail gets dumped right into the basket.

Wednesday, after picking up your dog at the vet, you received his annual dog tag and a rebate receipt for the heartworm medicine you recently bought. When you get home, the medicine, rebate form, receipt, and tag all go in the Sunday Basket. While you're making dinner, your daughter brings you a toy that needs new batteries. The toy gets dropped in the basket, too.

Thursday afternoon you pick up a card for your cousin's baby shower, which you are going to the following weekend, and drop off a shirt to be altered. The baby card, alteration ticket, and a recipe you tore out of a magazine are all dropped in the Sunday Basket.

Friday night you remember your parents' anniversary is in a few weeks. You jot down a note and drop it in the basket. Your kids clean out their backpacks, adding any papers for you to sign and school newsletters into the Sunday Basket. Your spouse grabs the receipts out of their car after work and drops those in your Sunday Basket, too.

On Sunday afternoon you brew your favorite herbal tea, grab your laptop, and get to work: opening mail, changing batteries, filling out forms, and paying bills. All those little tasks and to-dos are collected in this single place, to be tackled at this one time. At the end of ninety minutes your basket is empty and all the papers that can wait until next Sunday are filed in colorful slash pockets. (More on that soon.) You have a manageable list of items that will be done this week, and your family calendar is up-to-date.

You have given yourself grace and decided you can't do it all, but what you choose to do each week will be done with excellence. Your week feels less harried, and you notice an extra thirty to sixty minutes in your day during the workweek now that you have a place to defer actionable to-dos. You know that you can wait until Sunday—and, crucially, you know that you will actually get those tasks done. You are still using every minute of the day, but now you feel as though you are in charge of those minutes. Your smile is coming back, and your family is getting along better.

My Sunday Basket Story

Does this sound too good to be true?

It's not. This simple system works for me, and it will work for you, too. Let me tell you my story.

I created my first Sunday Basket many, many years ago, in a moment of desperation. I had too many papers in too many places (I hadn't yet perfected the art of the Big Purge as described in chapter 5!), bills were getting mislaid, business correspondence was going missing, and I was so overwhelmed that I was at my breaking point.

I was not sure how I was going to fix my problem, but I started by getting all my papers together in one place. I brought all my papers into the family room. Literally all of them. I had my business papers *plus* my kids' medical and adoption paperwork, and all the household to-dos and bills. I had sorted my mountains of paper and files into piles on every surface—the coffee table, TV stand, and fireplace hearth were covered in perfectly sorted stacks. But as soon as real life intervened (i.e., my kids came home), I needed a place for these piles to go.

I knew I needed to do something to keep the piles in check. I made several trips to office supply stores to find some way to get my paper organized. After trying several different products, I finally found what I call "slash pockets." These are plastic file folders with a slash across the front half. They have holes on one edge and tabs on the side like a regular binder divider. The slash pockets are great for corralling all those little loose papers into manageable chunks. I tossed them inside a decorative basket I already had in the house, and suddenly a lightbulb went off. The slash pockets let me organize the papers into easily accessible groups, they came in different colors (so I could color-code my papers), and if I put them in a box or basket, I could see the labels and not forget about a category of papers. You can find generic slash pockets in a variety of colors at any office supply store or online. You can also use regular old file folders in your Sunday Basket, too—I just happen to like the slash-pocket folders because papers seem to stay put a little better in those. (I also sell an Organize 365 Sunday Basket System online, and that includes all the necessary slash pockets described in this book.)

But I soon realized that although my papers were sorted by project, I still did not have a handle on what I needed to get done in a given week. I was still overwhelmed with leafing through dozens of different slash pockets every time I needed a piece of paper. So I decided to take a different approach.

That Sunday night, after the kids were in bed, I took out all my folders and sat on the floor with two baskets in front of me. One basket was to hold the papers and to-dos for that week, and the other one was to hold anything I did not need to do until the following Sunday.

I picked up each folder and asked myself, "Does this *need* to be done before next Sunday?" If it did, I put it in that week's basket. If not, it went in the other basket. Then, I tackled that week's to-do items and set aside the rest for another day.

Every Sunday, I would empty out my Sunday Basket. I would go through every loose paper and piece of mail and put it in an already established slash pocket. The big decision I needed to make was, "Is this something I need to deal with before next Sunday?" Any slash pocket that did not have something in it that needed to be done before next Sunday got put back in the Sunday Basket without getting completed. I called this "planned neglect." We cannot possibly follow through on every opportunity or idea in our lives. Information and paper come in so much faster than we can manage. The Sunday Basket allowed me to put aside current projects that I wanted to be working on for one week, but not lose track of the project. If I had extra time (*ha!*) or needed to work on the project earlier than planned, everything was together in the slash pocket and accessible if I needed it.

After much trial and error, I realized that the key to my sanity was making sure to go through everything in the Sunday Basket *every* Sunday. In order to stay organized, I need one day to deal with all the papers that accumulate over the week from the mail, school, work, and all the rest. Additionally, I realized that I needed a sacred time to plan my life and work for the upcoming week. I found the best day for me was Sunday, so I named my basket of papers **The Sunday Basket**. You need a day, too! For you it may be Monday, or Wednesday, or Friday. You can also use Sunday, too. I am willing to share!

If a paper or item needs attention in the current week, I leave it out until I have time planned to complete the task (to call for a doctor's appointment, to buy more toilet paper, to change a lightbulb, or to pay a bill that *has* to be done *this* week).

My Sunday Basket became the *one* home for all my active household papers, and I knew where to find them.

- *I had ideas for a business event in March, but it was January.*
- *I had pieces for a newsletter I was going to write in ten days.*
- *I had school forms for the kids to fill out that were due in two weeks.*
- *I had a flyer for summer camp that needed to be returned in April.*
- *I had ideas for posts for my blog.*
- *I had a flyer for an upcoming parenting seminar.*

- *I had received a new magazine in the mail.*
- *I had printed out articles to read for my kids' diagnoses.*
- *I had property tax bills due in June and September.*
- *I had the manual for a new appliance we bought that needed to be put away.*
- *I had a receipt for a shirt that did not fit and needed to be returned to the store.*

The key to the Sunday Basket is that you have to go through *everything* in the basket *every* Sunday.

The Sunday Basket helped me to restore my sanity and to keep my house free of loose paper clutter. My husband no longer saw paper piles a mile high. I could grab an item from the Sunday Basket and get it done. As I continued to use the Sunday Basket, I found myself dropping everything that could wait to be handled until Sunday into the basket. I could put the mail right in the Sunday Basket every day during the week and know I would handle it without missing anything.

The Sunday Basket frees your mind from worrying if things will get done and allows you to focus your time and energy on getting those things done. No matter how much you use digital systems, you cannot completely get away from paper. The Sunday Basket system will give you a place to store your paper and the organizational skills to ensure your papers get managed, not ignored.

The Sunday Basket helps to remove all the papers from the front of the refrigerator and the piles on the kitchen counter that are part of our day-to-day active papers. The Sunday Basket frees your mind from worrying that things will get done and allows you to focus your energy on what you *need* to get done.

So now I will help you build your first Sunday Basket. Read on!

How to Build Your Own Sunday Basket
Collect Your Active Papers

There are two ways to start your Sunday Basket. Many of my clients do not finish the Big Purge that you read about in the last chapter before they start their Sunday Basket. If that is an overwhelming task for you as well, feel free to jump right in and start with your Sunday Basket first. Others want to go through all their paper piles and files, do a Big Purge initially, and get a handle on their paper before setting up a Sunday Basket. Either way, grab a fresh bankers' box (remember those from chapter 5?), write "Sunday Basket" on the side in black Sharpie, and let's get started.

The easiest way to kick off the Sunday Basket process is to first gather all those loose papers on your kitchen counters and other living areas of your house. I want you to grab every piece of paper that's floating around your house—all your mail, permission slips, to-dos, the sports schedule on the fridge, and even items you are saving to read "later." Check your purse and wallet, too. Make sure you gather *everything*.

The Sunday Basket is going to be a place to keep all your active papers, and this bankers' box is your first starter Sunday Basket. If you are overwhelmed, I promise you that this is totally normal. You will progress to a cute "official" Sunday Basket as you get the backlog sorted and your Sunday Basket routine established. But to start, it is better to put everything you have not processed yet in one large holding pen. Your papers are safe in the bankers' box, and you have only one place to hunt for things if you need them before you establish your Sunday Basket routine.

Review Your Saved Papers

If you already did the Big Purge and you have a box (or boxes) of **Saved Papers** from that process, it's time to give them a closer look. Take all the papers out of the box and place them on a table. Are there active papers in there? Put them into your **Sunday Basket**. Are there papers you don't need to access for a while? Leave them in the **Saved Papers** box.

Each paper will either be a **Sunday Basket** paper or it will go back into the **Saved Papers** box for later review. Oh, and, yes, you can continue to recycle and shred paper at this point, too!

Remember: Sunday Basket = needs action or active. If it's not an active paper (i.e., you need it in the next four months), it doesn't belong in the Sunday Basket. By the time you're done with this process, you'll have a small pile of bills, notices, coupons, permission slips, and other time-sensitive papers in your Sunday Basket. So let's (finally) start organizing them.

Divide Papers into the Sunday Basket Slash Pockets

A warning: it will take about four to six weeks for your brain to be able to accept this new system and trust that you will not forget things. Trust this process, and give yourself grace. The

Sunday Basket is a representation of things you have not been able to get done yet. Do not make the mistake of thinking you will get this all done in a week and that you will be able to eliminate the basket.

Now we are going to sort your active Sunday Basket papers into the appropriate slash pockets. The transparent folders allow you to gather similar types of papers together. From many years of experience as a teacher and professional organizer, I have learned and confirmed that color-coding really does make a difference in the way our brains process information. I have assigned each slash-pocket color a specific task to help you learn my system.

I love slash pockets because they allow me to group all papers in one pocket, no matter what their size. With a file folder, smaller papers and note cards tend to fall out on three sides. The slash pocket does a much better job keeping my papers safe and inside the pocket. Additionally, since the slash pockets are transparent, I can see my notes and papers inside the pocket, which helps me to quickly identify the pocket I need or paper to retrieve.

I also love slash pockets because they are portable. It is easy to take a single slash pocket in the car to hold all the papers I need to complete my errand-running. I can take a stack of them to a client meeting to discuss all our active projects. And when I return home, I drop them back in the Sunday Basket and they are safe until the next Sunday. Finally, it is easy to move slash pockets in and out of my Sunday Basket depending on what is happening during the year. I can start a new one in January to collect my tax paperwork for the year. Or, if I finish my bathroom remodeling project, I can archive the necessary papers and use the slash pocket for my next adventure.

Here are five basic categories (coded by color) to get you started as you begin to organize your papers into those slash pockets. Note: not all of your papers will fall in these five categories. Projects, ideas, and long-range goals will be addressed in the next chapter.

Red = To Do This Week

Orange = Calendar and Computer

Yellow = Errands

Green = Money and Finances

Blue = Waiting For

The Red slash pocket will hold all the items that you know you need to do this week. Keep your planning sheet in this pocket. (More on the planning sheet on page 102.) Add in any loose papers that cannot wait until the following Sunday to be addressed. That way, when you have a few minutes to finish a task, you can grab the slash pocket and make progress. Ideally, you will also schedule some time to complete these must-do tasks on Sunday. Initially, this Red folder can also hold all the important, vital documents you discover as you sort through your paper. You will know where to find your birth certificates, passports, and similar items. Until you get all these squared away in their permanent homes, you will have one folder for safekeeping.

The Orange slash pocket is to hold all the papers and information that need to go on your calendar or in your computer. This includes dates to enter into your computer, weekly planning, registering for classes, or planning vacations. New sports schedules, wedding or party invitations, and the list of things you need to order from Amazon would all go in this folder. Sort all the appropriate paper into the Orange slash pocket while going through your loose Sunday Basket items, and then allow for some time at the end to take care of as many items as possible.

The Yellow slash pocket is for all the papers that you need to complete your errands. This is where you would put the dry-cleaning ticket, prescription scripts, forms for a doctor's appointment, coupons, shopping lists, or claim slips. One of my best time-management and organizing secrets is to schedule a regular errand day. This will optimize your productivity by completing as many errands as possible at the same time. Errand papers can include library book lists, putting a box of donations in the car, claim tickets for dry cleaning, receipts for returns, post office items, shopping lists, coupons, and anything else you need while out around town.

The Green slash pocket is the first holding place for any money- and finance-related items. You can put bills to pay (especially those weird bills like property taxes that come out so early), bank statements, or checks to cash in this pocket. It is also the place to put receipts, tax forms, financial statements, or requests for charitable donations. Again, I complete the items in this folder on Sunday.

The Blue slash pocket is a pending or tickler file. It will hold any reminders of things you are waiting for in your life. This can be the receipt for the Amazon order you made earlier, it may be a note to remind you that you are waiting for a friend to pick a date for dinner, you may be waiting to hear back about a reservation for a vacation, or you may be waiting for a rebate check. Other times, you may be waiting to hear back from someone you called or waiting for documentation. Put your reminders in this slash pocket, check it weekly, and follow up as needed.

Next, look at your calendar and decide *when* you will finish the items in the Red through Green slash pockets. Also decide *when* you will need to follow up on any items in the Blue pocket. You can make a to-do list for each day, or you can add the items as reminders on your Google Calendar, but make sure you will have enough time to do the tasks. Scheduling time to complete these items will help you be more realistic about how much you can do in a given week, and it will help you prioritize which things get done first. The longer you use your Sunday Basket, the more proactively you will be able to plan your life and the less reactive you will feel.

Complete Your To-Dos

I typically have one to two hours set aside for my Sunday Basket routine time each week. If I have had a crazy week, missed going through the basket for a week, or am anticipating having more than usual to tackle, I schedule extra time. If I am pressed for time, I sort more quickly and make sure that I identify all the must-do items for the week.

During my Sunday Basket time, I make sure to work through as many items as possible. In the beginning, it may take all your available time to just get through your active and incoming paperwork for the week. You will make your plan. But as you continue to stay organized and look forward in your calendar, you will gain breathing room. As I used the Sunday Basket regularly, I gained traction on my to-do items. Now I have more time to actually *finish* items during my Sunday Basket time.

I generally start with the items in the Orange pocket. I get all the new calendar items into my Google Calendar and make sure there are no conflicts for the week I have planned. I send calendar invitations to my husband as needed. I make sure that my kids have all their rides covered for the week, so I will often email the other family members who have been so generous to help us out. If I need to order things from Amazon, I start filling up my cart. I sometimes will open a cart at a big store like Walmart and start making a list for my next pickup. I typically wait until I have enough to meet the minimum for free shipping, but starting the list makes it easy to select for pickup if I need things sooner than I anticipated. If there are emails I need to send, library books to put on hold, or other computer work to do, I get it done.

The Blue pocket typically just requires a quick glance-through. For the most part, these items are just placeholders to make sure nothing slips through the cracks in our busy lives. If needed, spend a few minutes to check a tracking number or follow up on a refund that should have posted to your bank account. I recommend just making a note on the document with your follow-up as a reminder. If you find that you need to take care of an item during the week, schedule time on your calendar during business hours.

Next, I grab the Red pocket and work through as many to-do items as I can on Sunday. I fill out permission slips, deal with forms, read through fund-raiser order forms and make selections, prepare any birthday cards to mail out that week, and deal with any other pressing matters. Basically, if it needs to be done and does not fit into one of the other colors, it goes into my Red pocket and I get as much done as I can. Sometimes, I find that I get stuck on an item. Maybe I want to check with a friend to see if she is going to book club. Or I need to make a phone call but the office is closed. I try to make sure I have some time during the week (and ideally during the office workday) and block it out to finish my must-do tasks for this week. Develop a system that you know works for you. Will you take the slash pocket to work and get these done on your lunch break? Then put it in your work bag at the end of your Sunday Basket time. Do you work from home on Thursdays? Block out thirty to sixty minutes on your calendar so you can get this stuff done.

Then I grab my Green pocket and take care of any money and financial matters that can be handled on Sunday in the time I have left. I am working on automating my bill-pay systems, but I can write a few quick checks. I often grab and reconcile my medical insurance explanation of benefits with the bills from the medical providers. I still like to reconcile my checkbook, and will do that, too. Realistically, you may need to schedule a routine time on a different day to handle your financial paperwork. But by using the Sunday Basket, you will know you have triaged your money for the week and that all your paperwork is safe in one location.

My Yellow pocket is typically complete when my Sunday Basket has been completed and I put it in the car for the week. Every single week, I have items that need to be returned, donated, sold, fixed, or delivered. I make sure to put all the papers I need for errands inside. My slash pocket holds receipts for returns, coupons, shopping lists, and similar papers. I will put an errand list on a Post-it note or an index card and slip it inside the slash pocket so I do not forget any stops (post office, gas station, or prescriptions to pick up). I also put any physical objects that I can right into the car on Sunday night to get them out of the house and to have them ready so I can complete the errand. For example, when I needed to take a broken vacuum to a repair shop, I put it directly in the car. I was not sure exactly which day I would be able to drop it off, but I had it in the car, ready to go. Before I head out of the house, I look over my errand list. If I had another errand that brought me near the shop, I was ready to complete that errand.

I finish by setting up anything else I need to do to make my week successful. I restart and charge my electronics. I put any physical items needed for errands *in* the car (direct-sales items to drop off to clients, clothes to return to the store, or packages to mail at the post office). I also fill the medication boxes for every member of my family for the upcoming week. I make sure I have a plan for lunch for the next day (I often work from home, but this was *key* when my kids had to take lunch to school every day). And I am learning to set out my clothes and accessories for the next morning.

It sounds like a lot, but I have heard from so many of my clients just how freeing the structure of a Sunday Basket can be. My client Rachel sent me a quick email when she got home from her errand day: "Lisa, it's working!"

That morning her three errands turned into more with the regular unexpected events that come from being a mom, including going back home for items the kids forgot. However, it wasn't an issue. She had more than enough time to get it all done.

For years, Rachel had blamed her unpredictable retail schedule for why she "couldn't get it all done." With no two days looking the same, other attempts to implement schedules rarely made it past a few days.

She was honest with me that she never thought this would work for her and guarded her emotions for the inevitable failure this would be. Until it wasn't. Five weeks in, she had ditched her to-do list, and now she was getting more done than she ever thought possible.

"I have turned the corner from my old, reactive life, and I never want to go back!" she raved.

The Sunday Basket Routine

I love my Sunday evening routine. We have dinner as a family, then I do a series of weekly household chores (reboot and charge electronics, fill pill dispensers, and fold/put away laundry), take a nice long bubble bath, and thoroughly enjoy going through my Sunday Basket and planning my week. This is a process. The first six to eight weeks are going to be overwhelming. Your paper piles did not start yesterday, and they are not going to be gone tomorrow. However, each week you will feel more and more in control of your paper. In the meantime, you and your family will know where to find those active papers.

All week long, I toss everything into my Sunday Basket if it can wait until Sunday for me to look at it. I have put lightbulbs, door knobs, buttons for shirts, and grocery list items into the Sunday Basket. I also put ideas for episodes of my podcasts and birthday gifts in my Sunday Basket. I know that on Sunday, I will go through the Sunday Basket and every item will be addressed.

Each Sunday, gather up your Sunday Basket, your calendar, and your computer.

> **1.** Take everything out of your Sunday Basket and examine each loose paper or slash pocket. If it can wait until next Sunday, put it back in the Sunday Basket.

> **2.** If it needs to be handled this week, make sure you know when you are going to take care of the item or task. Do you need to go to a store? Do you need to research which item to buy online? Do you need to call and make an appointment? Do you need to figure out what size battery you need for your car key?

Before I consider my Sunday Basket "done," I grab my Yellow pocket and any items that need to be taken on errands that week (things like a package for the post office, the receipt and item to return to the store, and my reusable shopping bags and coupons for the grocery store) and put them in my car along with my errands slash pocket. Anything my family has not requested for errands by the end of Sunday will have to wait an additional week. This can be painful at first for other members of the family, but when the consequences are consistent, they learn to add their requests to the Sunday Basket.

I know that Sunday night works amazingly well for me, but what works for you? Although I highly recommend processing your Sunday Basket on Sunday, find a day of the week that works for your life schedule and your family. Especially if you do not work a traditional Monday-to-Friday job, you may find that a different day works well for you. The key is to pick a consistent day and time so that you will go through your Sunday Basket every week. Feel free to try different days and times. The most important thing is to keep your weekly habit in place once you choose a day and time.

Sunday Basket Planning Time

When I go through my Sunday Basket, I have my computer close by and I take a good look at the upcoming week on my Google Calendar. I use Google Calendar because it works for all the members of my family. If you do not have a calendar you already use and love, I recommend you explore Google Calendar and try this system. If you have a calendar system you use well, keep with what is working for you. This entire system is meant to be customized to your life.

If the week is particularly busy, I often write out my weekly schedule on a planning sheet. There's a blank copy for your use in the Appendix. You can also find a copy available for download at https://organize365.com/paperbookprintables.

Productivity experts show us that advance planning yields a four- to fivefold return on the time spent. The time I take to plan out my week and schedule my to-do tasks makes my week go so much more smoothly. I use my Sunday Basket time to look over my week and make my plan of what work I will get done and when I will be able to do it. I also look back at the last one to two weeks and make sure there is nothing leftover on my calendar. Sometimes looking at my old lunch plans with a friend reminds me to send her that book recommendation I promised. Or when I look back and see that I was at the dentist, I can make sure I put my new appointment in my calendar for next time. I also look ahead to the next two to four weeks. This helps me remember that our garbage pickup will be delayed by a day due to the holiday and that I need to put something for the bake sale on the grocery list.

For new users of the Sunday Basket system, I recommend writing out your schedule and to-do list. After using the Sunday Basket system for years, I have found that I no longer need a to-do list. I schedule time for my important tasks on my Google Calendar, and I can just grab the slash pocket for the scheduled time and get my work done.

Now I want to be honest with you here. There is still a limit to the hours you have in a given week. No matter how hard I try, I cannot seem to accomplish more than three priority tasks in a given day. I do not try to assign myself more than three combined work and home tasks each day. Usually I accomplish only one or two. If we try to squeeze everything in, nothing is a priority and our brains will clamor to keep our attention moving between hundreds of tasks, ideas, and items. As I plan my week, I try to anticipate when I can accomplish my priorities. I acknowledge these limitations and work within them. I focus on selecting the most important tasks that must get done for each day of the week. And then, as life happens, I adjust my plan depending on what life brings. If the kids get sick or my

	monday	tuesday	wednesday
Work Top 3			
Home Top 3			
7 a.m.			
8 a.m.			
9 a.m.			
10 a.m.			
11 a.m.			
12 p.m.			
1 p.m.			
2 p.m.			
3 p.m.			
4 p.m.			
5 p.m.			
6 p.m.			
7 p.m.			
8 p.m.			
9 p.m.			
Dinner			
Chores			

thursday	friday	saturday	sunday

planning time

Weekly Checklist Work To-Dos	Weekly Checklist Work To-Dos
☐ Pay bills and get out weekly cash	☐ _____ _____
☐ Reboot computer and cell phone	☐ _____ _____
☐ Email Inbox Zero (check text and FB messages)	☐ _____ _____
☐ Grocery	☐ _____ _____
☐ Meal planning	☐ _____ _____
☐ Laundry	
☐ Make an errand list	☐ _____ _____
☐ Go through the Sunday Basket	☐ _____ _____
☐ Plan my week	
☐ Place any online orders	☐ _____ _____
☐ Dry cleaning and prescriptions	☐ _____ _____
☐ Charge Apple watch, tablets, etc.	☐ _____ _____

website goes down, I compare my new to-do items to my old priorities and adjust. Progress, not perfection!

Sunday Basket FAQ

Q: Sunday will not work for me. Can I do the Sunday Basket on a different day?

A: Yes, of course you can pick a different day to work the weekly Sunday Basket system. The key is to pick the same day and time each week. The Sunday Basket system only works if you do it every week.

Q: My bills are paid online. How can I do this system if my bills are digital?

A: Most of my bills are automatically paid online as well. And I write very few checks. I still go through our weekly bank transactions online and plan out our next week's spending. This system gives me a placeholder to spend the time I need to take care of our family finances even if most of those are online.

Q: I have an online calendar. Why would I write out my weekly schedule on paper?

A: I too have an online calendar. The weekly planning portion of the Sunday Basket system allows your mind to replay the events of the previous week and think through any meetings, appointments, or events you completed that need follow-up on your calendar.

Likewise, looking forward to the following week allows you to see where you might need help with meal planning, carpooling, and meeting deadlines.

Q: Why don't you open your mail every day or at least recycle the junk?

A: I know it sounds crazy. I have analyzed home productivity for decades. I know what works for one family may not work for the next. Organization is a muscle. It is a skill that can be learned, and as you learn it, you will develop more tricks. Here is why I dump it all. . . .

Most people know the trick to recycle the junk mail and keep the good mail. That is a habit people try to implement, but it misses the goal. The goal is to process the *good* mail at least once a week. I have been in many homes with piles of non-junk mail never opened.

So I have you focus on the skill of putting *all* your mail in *one* place and processing it all at once one day a week. You don't need to put your junk mail in your Sunday Basket; I just know as soon as I start going through the mail and thinking about it, the time and stress savings of dumping it in the Sunday Basket is lost.

How Does the Sunday Basket Work with a Family?

First things first. Your Sunday Basket is just for you. Others can add items to your basket, but they shouldn't take them out unless you ask them to. Think of this like your inbox in a corporate office or the basket on your school teacher's desk where you submitted your work.

Naturally, as you start to use your Sunday Basket, your family will soon realize that if they want something to get on your list, they need to put it in the Sunday Basket. My kids know to drop their grocery requests and the mail right in my basket to be processed on Sunday.

Yesterday my daughter, Abby, asked me to program her car so the garage door code would work. I asked her to make me a note and put it in the Sunday Basket. In the past I would have said, "OK," and either forgotten to do it or had to stop what I was doing to figure that out. Now the task is recorded, and I will get to it when I can.

As a nice side note, sometimes my family will figure out, fix, or get what they need themselves, now that they know my daily plan doesn't stop for every single request that is made of me.

Making Progress

For the first six weeks of going through your Sunday Basket, I want you to triage your papers. I tell you to ask yourself, "Can this wait until next Sunday?" and if the answer is yes, I want you to put the piece of paper, slash pocket, or item back in the basket. When you are digging out from a lifetime of disorganization, this is a vital approach to prioritization. You *must* choose the most urgent and important tasks to focus on first, or you will not learn to trust and use your system.

Do not worry about when it will get done, how it will get

done, or who will do it. We are triaging your paper pile like an ER nurse would triage patients. What can wait? Everything that can wait must wait. Too often we look at all of our to-dos and start to prioritize. There is not a single person on this planet who can do everything, and do it well.

As you continue to use and work deeper into your Sunday Basket, you may want to consider a slightly different question. Instead, ask yourself, "What can I do this week to make progress on my goals?" Or, "What can I do this week to make my future better?" Or, "What am I inspired to complete this week?" As you use your Sunday Basket to pursue your unique purpose in life, consider how you spend your time and what it says about your life priorities. As you set up your calendar, consider how much time you have to dedicate to your goals this week. Think about how you can declutter your calendar and make more time for the things that truly matter to *you*.

The Sunday Basket helps to remove mile-high papers from every flat surface in your home. You can grab a single slash pocket and move forward on a paper or project. If you are ambitious, you can sort your mail into the appropriate Sunday Basket folders each day as it arrives. But most important, your Sunday Basket will free your mind from worrying that things are undone. You will better focus your energy on what you need to get done.

The Sunday Basket is also successful at changing how we deal with paper, because it really is a weekly planning session that lasts about ninety minutes. When the Sunday Basket is fully completed, bills are paid, the week is planned in advance (and any upcoming needs like transportation, food, gifts, and clothing are prepared), our brain can begin to rest, knowing we have a system to take care of all the things it otherwise felt responsible for reminding us to do, usually at the worst time. Really, brain? Why do you only remind me to replace the smoke detector battery when I am lying in bed nearly asleep? Even better, the Sunday Basket helps us to be realistic about how much time we have and what we can accomplish.

As you work the Sunday Basket system, you will find that you are able to clear out the flood of papers that has accumulated on your counters and tables. The chaos will diminish. And you will find that you have slightly more time, energy, and focus. This most typically happens after using the Sunday Basket for about six weeks. At that time, you'll begin to layer in time to work on your next-level projects—what I call your Sunday Basket 2.0—or to work ahead on things you now know and remember are coming in the future. After you complete all the things that must be done this week, start to think about what *else* you want to move forward in your life. You still need to decide what your own life priorities are and what will receive your energy. And for that we need to move to the next level of organizing your Sunday Basket, the twenty 2.0 slash pockets that hold your passions, projects, and future dreams.

CHAPTER 7

Customize Your Sunday Basket

How to Modify the Sunday Basket for *Your* Life

FACT: 95 percent of all information is still processed in paper form, with employees printing an average of forty-five sheets of paper per day.

(Frank Booty, *Facilities Management Handbook,* Burlington, MA: Elsevier/ Butterworth-Heinemann, 2006)

Before my client Holly started her Sunday Basket, she had piles of unread mail—and it was stressing her out. She explained to me that between her full-time corporate job and a busy two-year-old daughter, she was running from morning until night—constantly in reactive mode rather than proactively getting ahead of her personal papers. "I found myself spending valuable weekend time going through piles of credit card offers and paging through catalogs—then running out of time before I got to the actual bills I needed to pay!" she recounted. Her to-do list and folders she didn't want to deal with would be forgotten until they were past due and irrelevant.

"After starting the Sunday Basket, I now know where everything actionable lives," she explained. "I have a dedicated time to go through it weekly. And weirdly, this regimented system has allowed me to be a much more creative person! I expected to get my daily kitchen pile under control, but the extra time I found has been an unexpected gift. I actually found time to do some creative journaling every morning!"

The Sunday Basket is a place to collect any and all ideas you have during a week. Writing something down and dropping it in your Sunday Basket is not a commitment until you decide that it is. You can cancel or discard any item in the box at any time. You can even discard a full project slash pocket at any point in this process. The Sunday Basket is meant to help you be organized, but it is not the boss of you.

After six to eight weeks of using the Sunday Basket system, you will be amazed at how much better you are at managing your active papers. Your bills will be paid on time, and you will have a better handle on where your money is going. You will be on time, and you'll be surprised to find that you have not missed an appointment in weeks. You'll still have a ton to do, but you will start to feel as though you have some control of your paper. But by this point, you'll also find some holes in the system.

Those slash-pocket folders you set up at first are great for short- and medium-term projects. But most likely, you are noticing that you had a bunch of intangible ideas, plans for the future, notes to yourself, and other papers that are left over in your Sunday Basket but do not *need* to be done that week. Maybe there's a big home reno project that you're planning. Or a vacation that you're starting to think about. The good news is that your Sunday Basket can be customized and refined to work for you and your life. I call this the Sunday Basket 2.0.

More Pockets to Customize Your Sunday Basket

You'll remember that the original Sunday Basket you set up in chapter 6 had five color-coded folders or slash pockets: Red (to-do this week), Orange (calendar and computer items), Yellow (errands), Green (money and finances), and Blue (waiting for/pending items). Now that you've got those basic categories up and running, you can add more folders into the mix. Each new folder represents a specific goal or an active project, and you'll keep them alongside the original folders in your Sunday Basket.

The additional colors of folders you'll be using to add to your Sunday Basket are Pink (personal), Purple (home), Blue (family), and Green (money). Wait, didn't we already have Green and Blue folders? Yes, but these are two areas (money and general to-do/pending items) that often benefit from this additional customization, and that's where the 2.0 made-to-order folders come in. So, for example, you may wish to have one Green folder for coupons and another Green folder for receipts. Or one of your big "pending" items might be vacation planning—that can get its own Blue folder. Think of these additional categories as your Sunday Basket "expansion set" that allows you to tailor your Sunday Basket to your home, your goals, and your life.

A word about the additional 2.0 category colors I've suggested: these colors (Pink for personal items, Purple for home items, etc.) seem arbitrary, and in many ways they are. But they also match the colors of the Organize 365 Sunday Basket sys-

tem I sell on my website, and the color categories I often reference on my podcast, my online classes, and in all my course
materials. Do you need to buy my branded products to make
the Sunday Basket work for you? Absolutely not. But I do recommend you try to find folders or slash pockets that match the
colors I reference in this book if at all possible—I'll be refer-
ring to the categories by color at other places throughout this
book, and it helps avoid confusion if you have your Sunday
Basket organized by roughly the same color scheme.

Remember: your Sunday Basket is totally customizable, but
here are some suggestions for additional slash pockets.

PINK = PERSONAL	PURPLE = HOME
Wardrobe needs	Car
Volunteer activity	Chores
Meal plan	Cleaning schedule
Exercise program	Memorabilia
Travel goals	Papers to file
Spiritual notes	Remodeling ideas
BLUE = FAMILY	**GREEN = MONEY AND FINANCE**
Family members by name	Budget
Holiday	Coupons
Graduation	Items to sell (listed for sale)
Pets	Philanthropy
Summer camp	Receipts
Vacation	Taxes
Date-night ideas	Bank statements

These additional slash pockets are intended to be tools to
help you keep track of the small, fiddly to-do items on your
list that can easily get lost or overlooked. Look at these categories and, if they apply to you and your to-do items, make

appropriate slash pockets to match them. And if you have other categories that aren't covered here, feel free to make a slash pocket for them, too! This is where you start to customize this system to fit your family and your life.

One of the ways you can use your slash pockets is to make specific folders for family members or important people in your life. You can include notes about information you want to discuss. For example, you can drop questions to ask the doctor, topics to ask the accountant, gift ideas, or possible vacation destinations. When you do get some time together, you can sit down and make sure to discuss the most pressing topics. In the pages that follow, I'll show you how I and many of my clients set up and use other customizable slash-pocket folders in our Sunday Baskets.

Another important note: you will probably *not* need all these additional folders in your Sunday Basket! You never manage to redeem your coupons? Don't create a slash pocket for them—after all, keeping more paper that you never use is the antithesis of the Paper Solution! And of course, more slash pockets mean more to-do items. But don't let this overwhelm you. As you work your way through your Sunday Basket every week, you will get better at estimating how much work you can get done in a week. You will sometimes find that your week gets busy and you do not make it through all your planned work. However, you will always know where your papers are, and you will have determined your priorities for the week—and you will be able to pivot with the realities of life.

The reality is that most of us can handle only five to fifteen ongoing projects at one time. Having a limited number of *active* slash pockets helps you to be realistic about how many things you are trying to accomplish at one time. The beauty of the slash-pocket system is that you can pause a project and keep your papers organized even when they are not active. You are not required to discard things; instead, you can put them on hold if other life priorities arise.

Are there projects on your wish list that might need their own pocket? What category would they fall into?

Plan Your Three "New" Years

Over time I have come to experience and observe that many of us are trying to plan and run our home life based on the quarterly and annual corporation method. For years I tried to get my life to work in twelve-week quarters, to no avail. July 1 is smack in the middle of summer. October 1 comes right as I am hitting the middle of my most productive time of year, September 1 to late November.

After much trial and error, I determined I actually prefer dividing my year into three planning and productivity cycles, not four. Embracing these three cycles has freed me from unrealistic goals and helped me achieve different kinds of goals in different seasons.

All household goals are not created equally. Some, like home improvement and teaching life skills to kids, are done quicker and easier in the summer. Others, like detailed crafting and paper organization, are done more easily in the winter, when we spend more time inside. And big transformational mental projects, like writing a book, organizing the whole house, and reworking your business plan, are done in the fall.

I have named these cycles my Three New Years: New Year

(January through May), Summer (June through August), and the School Year (September through December). At the start of each of these "years," I make time for an extended planning session and clean out my Sunday Basket from past projects and goals.

Additionally, I take a good look at the next "year" and call ahead to schedule appointments we will need during that time. Honestly, I hate taking half a day to call for appointments and book the calendar, but I am always so glad when it is done. Plus, I find that I have better options for appointment times and a more reasonable schedule when I plan in advance.

Appointments I bulk-schedule include:

- *Dog boarding dates*
- *Haircuts*
- *Physicals*
- *Other annual doctors' appointments*
- *Dentist appointments*
- *Household services and maintenance*
- *Vacations and travel arrangements*
- *Babysitters*
- *Camp registrations*
- *School meetings*
- *School events*
- *Car maintenance and oil changes*

Often after I finish my marathon scheduling session, I find that I am left with a pile of papers that I will need for the appointments. There may be back-to-school physical forms, or I may need to fill out a health history for summer camp. Rather than having to search all over the house or dig through piles on the morning of the appointment, I put the papers in my Sunday Basket errand slash pocket. If you use an electronic calendar like Google, you can also put a note on the appointment in your calendar to remind you where you "filed" the papers in your Sunday Basket. This can help you remember to actually take the papers to the appointment!

One of the reasons I divide up the year into three "new year" segments is that I get to start over more often. Looking over all my slash-pocket labels at least three times a year, especially those longer-term projects that I may not touch every week, re-prioritizes my time and helps me achieve my goals. You can use this time to evaluate if you are still interested in and committed to the project listed on the slash pocket. If you had a slash pocket for a household project that has been completed (like redoing your closet), move the reference papers to archive/reference binders (more on those in a bit) and remove the rest. If you are no longer interested in working on a given project, clear out the pocket and make it available for a new project.

The most freeing part of this process is that I can change my mind. What felt so important and "had to be done" just a few months earlier can be let go without guilt now, knowing it wasn't the right season for that project. When your Sunday Basket gets too full of project goals and opportunities, I give you permission to delete, defer, and delegate those slash pockets. Getting organized is as much about deciding what you want as it is getting it done.

The Sunday Basket is a holding place for all those actionable to-dos and projects. *You* get to decide when and if they get done. Just because they made it into the basket doesn't mean you have to do them. Each week different priorities will surface and make it on your weekly calendar—and the rest can wait.

Make It a Habit

The key to a successful Sunday Basket is to use it *every single week*. It will take a while to train your family to put important papers into your Sunday Basket. You must persevere. One loose paper becomes a mountain just like one unwashed glass becomes a sink full of dishes. Both must be maintained.

One of the most important habits you will develop is when papers come into your house, put *everything* that can wait until next Sunday in your Sunday Basket. We are constantly trying to remember things and constantly trying to stay on top of things. The Sunday Basket is a *huge* help here. Personally, I like to make notes and jot down ideas all through the week and then go through them all together on a Sunday. I find 50 percent of the items in my Sunday Basket are notes to myself. This really works for me. I make the notes all week long, and my brain can focus on my family and my work because it can trust that I will handle the important things at the appropriate time.

The second important habit is creating the routine of using the Sunday Basket on a regular basis every week. The real secret to the Sunday Basket is the consistent review of our papers and the progress we make on getting things off our to-do lists. Consistency is the key to success, but it can be hard to get used to building in time for a regular Sunday Basket session. In the past, I set up filing systems and then promptly forgot where I filed something. Because you keep your Sunday Basket on the kitchen counter, you will *never* forget to use it. The closer and easier your system is, the more you will use it and love it. It will take some time to build your habit of clearing out your Sunday Basket and planning your week, but this is a much more sustainable habit.

Developing new habits is a challenge for almost all of us. Adding new steps to our daily and weekly routines requires vigilance and discipline. For those of us with a long history of disorganization, trying to establish new habits can be discouraging.

Here are some suggestions to build the habit:

1. Same time, same day, each week. When do you brush your teeth? Do your weekly grocery shopping? Get your weekly cash out of the bank? For each of these items where a time popped into your head, you have created a habit. Habits have a routine time they are done. Your Sunday Basket needs a day and time to become a successful habit.

2. Set a phone alarm for your planned Sunday Basket time. Until your Sunday Basket time is a habit, you can set a weekly reminder on your phone to hold you accountable and remind you to do your new habit. You may have to try out a few different days and times to find the one that works best for you and your family. Once you find a winner, stick with that same day and time!

3. **Leave yourself a fun surprise inside the Sunday Basket.** Maybe a gift card, favorite snack, or other treat. Who doesn't like a treat! Rewards work! Drop in a reminder note to have a nice Sunday night cocktail, special dessert, walk after dinner, or just the accomplished feeling of a job well done. What treats do you like to work for? Build in a reward you give yourself when your weekly Sunday Basket time is over.

4. **As you look at your calendar for next week, if you absolutely cannot make your Sunday Basket appointment time, set an alternate time in stone and make sure you get your papers cared for.** While the goal is to do your Sunday Basket each week on Sunday, life will get in the way. Make a plan for the unexpected, and work your plan. The benefits of building your new habit will far outweigh skipping a week.

The Most Common Papers in Your Sunday Basket

I will *always* encourage you to adapt your Sunday Basket to your paper, life, and home. However, here are some recommendations for common types of paper you will find in your Sunday Basket.

TRUST THE SYSTEM

This system works! After working with thousands of clients over many years, I have found that most people need about six weeks to develop an effective Sunday Basket habit. Remember, organization is a skill, and it can be taught. Over these six weeks, you'll start to learn the basics of paper organization and how to incorporate this new method into your busy life. It won't happen overnight! Learning this skill requires time, but by condensing that time into one period once a week, it becomes manageable.

But just like any other skill, paper organization also requires a little practice. The first few weeks have the heaviest load of paper sorting and decision making. The longer you work your Sunday Basket system, the further in advance you will be able to anticipate, plan, and make decisions. Funny enough, you probably will not even realize how much your Sunday Basket is keeping you organized until you miss a week and experience how life used to be.

Bills

As you sort your mail and find your bills to pay, you can know they rest safely in your Sunday Basket. If you have a typical household, you can likely get away with one Green bill-pay slash pocket. If you have a business with expenses to document or if you have many medical expenses or insurance documents to track, you may want separate folders. If you keep a written or printed copy of your budget, it can also live in a Green slash pocket.

Use your Green bill-pay slash pocket to keep all your incoming bills. When you open your bills, touch each piece of paper and make decisions about your financial situation. Depending on how much financial juggling you need to do, you can decide week to week which bills to pay. If it is not time to deal with a particular bill, put it back until the next week. If you keep a spreadsheet for taxes for medical, charity, or work receipts, you can keep that in your Green slash pocket, too.

I recommend using a spreadsheet of your regular (monthly) and irregular (property tax, insurance, school fees) bills that you keep in your Sunday Basket. I offer my clients a monthly bill-pay list that's also in the Appendix. I use mine by listing each bill in order by the due date and then highlight them after I send in the payment. This was especially important early in my marriage, when my husband's and my finances were leaner. Each time our family got paid income, we started with the bills that *had* to be paid, and it helped our family know when my variable income needed to be less variable and more income.

When you find yourself tempted to keep paid bills (especially those more than a year old), really ask yourself, "*Why* would I need this?" If you do not have a solid, reasonable answer, toss it!

Receipts

In every house I have organized, I have found piles of receipts. The questions were always: Do we need them? And, if we keep them, how do we organize receipts?

First, consider receipts for purchases under $100. Receipts are to provide a proof of purchase. If you do not check your receipts against a statement or do not plan to return an item, there is no reason to save them.

For store returns, *most* stores can look up your purchase by the credit card you used when you bought the item. If you pay cash, you may need to keep the receipt slightly longer in case you need to return a broken or unwanted item. My best advice is not to buy anything you think you might return. If you find that you have a history of shopping for "retail therapy" or you have bought a bunch of things you have never used, make a commitment to buy less. You can try something like delaying any purchases *not* on a list for at least thirty days. Or you can do a buy-nothing (sometimes called a "no spend") month.

You can sometimes watch me deal with unwanted purchases on my Insta Stories or on Facebook. I can often be seen just donating things I buy that do not work in my home. For smaller purchases, if I do not want to keep something, I just get it out of my home. It is rarely worth my time to keep track of a receipt and go back to the store for an item that cost less than $10.

During the week, I toss receipts into my Sunday Basket. Each Sunday, I reconcile my receipts to my checkbook or on-line bank account (I hear from so many of you who no longer reconcile checkbooks that I am ready to try letting it go). Then I shred or throw away the receipts. I live on the edge like that.

If you want to save *all* your receipts, knock yourself out. I recommend using slash pockets to do so. I find that three months is usually enough, but if you want to keep a full year, be

monthly checklist

Home Checklist

- ☐ Change furnace filter
- ☐ Change vacuum bag
- ☐ Check cleaning supplies
- ☐ Disinfect trash can
- ☐ Clean microwave
- ☐ Wash washing machine
- ☐ Flush garbage disposal
- ☐ Clean oven
- ☐ Clean out fridge/freezer
- ☐ Wash and clean out car
- ☐ Change bed sheets

Family Management

- ☐ Check for birthdays/holidays
- ☐ 15th reconcile checkbook
- ☐ Place order for paper products/monthly recurring
- ☐ Order prescriptions
- ☐ Check family bathroom supplies
- ☐ Check monthly lunch account balance
- ☐ Schedule doctors' appointments
- ☐ Schedule haircuts

Pets

- ☐ Flea, tick, and heartworm meds
- ☐ Wash bowls

Date	Bill	Amount

sure to get twelve slash pockets. Keep the slash pocket for the current month in the Sunday Basket and add receipts each week as you go through your Sunday Basket. You can print out receipts from online purchases and add them to the slash pocket, too. When you have full slash pockets from the three previous months, go through the oldest receipts, file them in your binders, and discard (shred or recycle) the rest. Then you have an empty slash pocket for the current month and can begin collecting the receipts again.

For major purchases like appliances or home improvements, I add my receipts to the appropriate binder.

Coupons

If you still collect and use paper coupons, the best way to manage them is to be choosy about which coupons you keep. I know, it's so hard to throw away free money. However, companies *want* coupons to be hard to organize and use so they do not lose money. If a coupon sits in your slash pocket for weeks or months, does it really matter? They are out of the way, and you can find them if you need them. At the same time, carefully consider what you actually save by using coupons, and determine if it is a good return on your time, energy, and paper-organizing space. I also recommend considering electronic coupon apps rather than keeping them on paper.

If you are committed to *using* paper coupons (not just collecting them), you can dedicate a Blue (family) or Purple (home) slash pocket to holding them. Each week as you make your shopping list and errands list, go through your coupon stash and add any relevant coupons to your Yellow errands slash pocket. Also, make sure you go through your coupons regularly to clean out any that have expired.

Projects

The Sunday Basket really shines when it comes to organizing papers for projects. Projects can have an end date or be ongoing. Each of the slash pockets can be designated for a project. Using your preferred color-coding system, designate a slash pocket to each project. You can make your slash-pocket categories as broad or as narrow as makes sense to your brain. For example, you could choose to have one slash pocket for your kitchen remodel, or you could have several different slash pockets with detailed categories like appliances, layout, flooring, cabinets, and contracts.

Slash pockets are perfect for project organization because they easily hold to-do lists, Post-it notes, index cards, décor samples, computer printouts, receipts, notebook pages, and all kinds of documents for your project that you want kept together. After you complete your project, you can determine *what* pages you need to keep, file those in the appropriate binder (see Part III), and then use the slash pocket for the next project.

Tickets

When you sign up for a class or get tickets for an event, where do you keep the receipt or the tickets until the event actually occurs? In your Sunday Basket, of course! But more specifically, if you have only a few items, you can keep them in the Blue waiting for/pending folder. Or, if it makes sense for you, you can also keep them in your Orange calendar folder. Either choice is fine—just decide and be consistent! If you have a more frequent need for tickets for something like regular travel or a theater subscription, you can dedicate a slash pocket to that event. Also, be sure to put the event on your calendar, and consider leaving a note in the digital event to remind yourself where to find your tickets.

Travel

For a single upcoming trip, I recommend an individual slash pocket for each trip. You can choose a color that is related to the person or persons involved in the trip. If you are traveling solo, it is likely best to use a Pink slash pocket. For a family trip, choose a Blue one. Start the slash pocket when you begin to daydream and research the trip. As you make decisions and reservations, you can eliminate the pages you have decided *not* to use. For example, you may start by printing the first page of several hotels that look interesting. Once you book your reservation, get rid of the rest. If you ever plan a future trip to the same area, you will almost always do a new internet search for area hotels.

As you get closer to your trip, you may want to designate a separate, short-term box for your travel. You may want to divide your paperwork into slash pockets for different information, like transportation (flight or road trip itinerary), lodging, meals, activities, or conference registration information. My family travels to Florida every summer, and in the spring, I begin to gather things in my travel box. I use my box to store magazines and catalogs to read, small toys or treats for the kids, work I want to take along, and I sometimes make a checklist of things I can do in the car, like update my phone, cull contacts, fill out financial spreadsheets, or organize photos on my phone or computer.

Forms

If you are an adult human living on planet Earth, you have forms to fill out. If you have kids, you have even more. In one week, I had to fill out new patient papers for a child's allergy testing, complete a high school application form, submit two out-of-network insurance claims, and sign a child up for a sports team. It took two hours just to handle the forms.

Paperwork like this eats up your time, but it is rare that we plan or account for this kind of life work. As much as possible, drop the forms you receive during a week into your Sunday Basket, and fill them all out at once; this is a type of task-batching that can help you be more productive. You can sit down and let your brain focus on the act of filling out forms all at the same time. If you need to look up information to fill out the forms, you only have to take out your reference binders once and put them away once.

Here are some additional ways to use the Sunday Basket to save time filling out forms:

- *Have extra copies of your child's birth certificate in the reference binders so you do not need to make copies to submit forms.*
- *Take the time to put your preferred pharmacy into your cell phone and write it in your Medical Organizing binder.*

- *Consider adding your child's Social Security number as a contact in your phone, but disguise it or alter some of the numbers.*
- *Enter your insurance information as a phone contact.*
- *Add your doctors' contact information, including address and phone, into your phone contacts.*

To-Do List

Several years after I started my Sunday Basket, I realized I no longer used a to-do list. I have found that I write notes to myself on index cards and toss them into my Sunday Basket. If you run across a friend who asks for a book recommendation, drop a note into your Sunday Basket. When you remember an item you need to pick up at the store or order online, stick a note in your Sunday Basket. If you have a project that needs to be done (landscaping the yard, planning a birthday party, or buying a new car), start with dropping your thoughts into your Sunday Basket. As you go through the items each week, you will block out calendar time to get them done. As you mentally commit to working through different projects, assign the project a slash pocket, and each week you will review your list and decide what things will receive your time and attention that week.

Correspondence

The Sunday Basket is also a great place to store and remember to check for correspondence. You can keep birthday cards or blank cards to send to friends and family for birthdays, anniversaries, or other special events. The Household Operations Binder (more on this later) has a list of important days and events. You can keep a copy in your Sunday Basket, and it will help you to send cards on time. When you think of something you want to acknowledge for a friend, drop a note in your Sunday Basket and write out a card during your Sunday Basket time. Some of my team members keep blank cards, stamps, and return labels in a special slash pocket for correspondence.

Kids' Paper

If you are in the stage of life where you are responsible for your children's paper, you can manage that in the Sunday Basket, as well. Each member of your family should have his or her own Blue (family) slash pocket. This individual slash pocket is the best place to keep those flyers, permission slips, book order forms, money requests, or other paperwork from week to week. Within the slash pocket, I recommend you use a highlighter to mark any dates or money that is due. As you highlight, also add the events and due dates to your master calendar. Within the slash pocket, it works best to stack the papers with the first to occur or be due on top, and the last to occur or be due on the bottom. That way, during a super hectic week when you need to cut short your Sunday Basket time, you can glance at the top page and put the whole slash pocket back in the Sunday Basket if nothing needs to be done that week. Kids' slash pockets are also a safe and reliable place to keep reading logs, passwords, or other child-specific information. The longer you use the Sunday Basket, the more reliable your paper-organizing system will become.

Major Projects (Hint: Get an Extra Box)

As previously discussed for travel, there are times when you will find it most helpful to just designate a whole box for a project. As your project grows, you may not be able to keep all the papers and parts in your Sunday Basket without overwhelming it. At those times, you may want to start a separate box for the different roles or projects in your life. **The longer you use the boxes and slash pockets to keep your ideas and thought processes organized, the faster and easier it will be to complete your projects.** This works because in the Sunday Basket system, I am not just suggesting organizing items (like those slash pockets); I'm also teaching you the skills and systems of being organized.

Here are some projects you may want to consider separating out into specific boxes:

- *Travel, especially large trips*
- *Home renovations*
- *Home decoration*
- *Party planning*
- *Major life events—graduation, going to college, finding a job*
- *Holidays*
- *Weddings*
- *Adding children to your family*

Once you learn the skills from the Sunday Basket, you will likely find that you also need a similar system to organize your work papers. When you understand this basic system, you might also want to customize an organizing box for:

- *Teachers and school administrators*
- *Homeschooling families*
- *Entrepreneurs and small-business owners*
- *Direct sales and franchisees*
- *Professional organizers*
- *Real estate professionals*
- *Corporate workers*
- *Volunteer leaders (coaches, Scout leaders, church leaders, etc.)*

If you do opt to use multiple baskets—and I have been using two to four Sunday Baskets and work boxes for over a year!—you *must* have a regular time to process the contents of your baskets. Most of the time, I spend four to six hours on Sunday and go through all the boxes in my life in one big work and planning session. At other times, it has made more sense to go through my work boxes during my workday on Friday, and I take care of my Sunday Basket and homeschool papers over the weekend. Anytime is the right time as long as you build the habit and go through your papers *every* week.

The Power of an Unencumbered Mind

What's the result of all this time you'll gain from purging your excess papers, creating your Sunday Basket, and then using that to organize your calendar and schedule? I'd argue that the benefit is bigger and more significant than just "organization."

The Sunday Basket is something I created out of desperation and then refined over time. I knew it helped me, and as I started teaching the system to clients and sharing my organization methods more widely over the past several years, I've seen the profound impact it can have on others' lives, as well. One of my clients, Holly Knill, is a Licensed Clinical Professional Counselor, and she reached out to tell me how much the Sunday Basket system has helped her—and why she thinks it actually clicks with people from a neuroscientific perspective.

Holly said, "Neuroscience has discovered that our mind at rest is still always thinking and, left to its own devices, it goes into a Default Thinking Mode." Default Thinking Mode is a largely unconscious type of brain activity in which we ruminate repeatedly about the past, the future, our worries, or our anxieties. Think of it as a running to-do list that you're constantly fretting over. "Scientists have found this 'default mode' is more active when people are depressed," Holly explained.

But thankfully, we can pull ourselves out of default mode into a more task-oriented headspace—getting past simple rumination into problem solving and decision making. "The Sunday Basket is a tool to help your brain switch into task-oriented mode," said Holly. "Basically, the Sunday Basket is supported by neuroscience to help reduce depression and depressive feelings. It's effective because it works with the way we are wired, rather than trying to fit ourselves into our perfectionistic view of what our homes 'should' look like and how we 'should' operate."

Basically, by off-loading an ongoing to-do list from your brain into the Sunday Basket (where you know it will be seen and dealt with in due course), you can reduce how much time you waste, eliminate guilt and stress, and actually clear more space in your brain to tackle what really matters to you.

Depression

Though I did not talk about it for many years and kept the knowledge very private, I struggled with depression in my own life. And as you might expect, I worked with many clients with depression over the years—some active and some who had found recovery.

Initially, I found the fact that I was facing depression fairly surprising. Juggling home, work, and kids, I never stopped moving. Every ad I saw for depression medication showed a woman who couldn't get out of bed—that wasn't my life. I couldn't get *into* bed—I had too much to do! Bills I couldn't pay, doctors' appointments too important to miss, extended family to care for, laundry piled high with no clean underwear in sight, and we were running low on toilet paper. Through it all, I kept moving. So I didn't think I was depressed.

I remember the day I finally lost it. It wasn't the day my dad died. Or the day I met the third lawyer. Or even when the ambulance was called for one of my kids.

No, it was in the drive-through lane at Walgreens.

I was picking up one of our eighteen monthly medications, and I had figured out if I kept switching pharmacies (who has time for that?!) I would get $25 coupons to help pay for the medication my family's lives depended on. And the teller wouldn't take my coupon.

I was tens of thousands of dollars in debt, sleep-deprived beyond belief, with no idea how to solve any of our family's real problems . . . and I lost it on that poor teller.

And I mean *lost it*. Screaming, crying, rationalizing, pleading. Lost it. And no, I didn't get the coupon. I drove home thinking, *What is the matter with me?*

I knew this wasn't right, but I had no idea how to fix it. Life didn't feel fixable. I couldn't see a way out.

A month later, when I was sick and at the doctor's office, I asked for an antidepressant. My physician a year prior didn't think I needed one. That physician also wanted me to come back for a second appointment to get a prescription. She had a one-malady-at-a-time policy. I didn't have the time, so I never made that appointment.

Luckily, this nurse practitioner didn't mind when I asked for an antidepressant at my sick visit. I felt as though I cheated, but I didn't know what else to do. I started the pills the next day. A year later, I was feeling more myself. Shortly after that, I started tackling my own personal paper tsunami. And today, I have developed the tools that I'm sharing with you.

Here are five tips I gave myself and share with clients about how depression affects organization.

1. Give yourself grace. I cannot even put into words how depression zapped me of every shred of energy to do *anything*. And the thought of tackling an organization project was so overwhelming. My willpower got up and went *away*!

2. Get a friend to help you. A friend's perspective, energy, and motivation are contagious and can help you push through when you just want to watch TV. Friends can help you get organized and stay functioning when your own initiative is low. Back when I led a home organizing team, over 50 percent of our Organize 365 clients called us in to help because they just could not do the organizing themselves in their depressed state. People found that they needed help with both physical clutter and paper organizing as they worked on their mental health.

3. Pick one area and complete it before moving on, no matter how long it takes. Slow and steady wins the race! Your papers did not become a mess overnight, and they will not get organized overnight, either. One step at a time. Pick an area where you can get a quick win and start there. Put all the mail together in a laundry basket. Open all the mail and throw out the envelopes. Get rid of any catalog more than thirty days old. And when you are done for the day, take the recycling out of the home. The key is to *maintain* that area when you tackle the next area. This book will help you move through your paper in an organized fashion, and you will continue to work toward an organized home and life.

4. Acknowledge your limitations. I know how frustrated you are! Knowing what I *used* to be able to do made me even *more* depressed when I couldn't seem to tackle even the basics. If it is a bad day, that's OK! You will have time to get organized. First, take care of yourself. And when your desire is beyond your physical ability, save up and hire help. Find someone you trust, especially with the private, sensitive information that is in your paper. If you need us, Organize 365 offers live paper-organizing retreats where we will help you in person.

5. Surround yourself with positive people. I know it is easier to say than do, but I always felt better when I made myself go *out* and *be* with people, even though I did not want to. I cannot tell you how many times I would be laughing with clients and then they would say:

- *"I can't believe how fun you make organizing!"*
- *"I haven't been able to laugh like that in a long time."*
- *"If I knew how quickly you could get this organized, I wouldn't have waited so long to call."*
- *And my favorite: "I can't believe there are people who actually like to organize!"*

If you have ever experienced depression or anxiety, you know that your brain begins to be less effective. There's so much to keep track of in our lives: the paperwork, the house maintenance, schedules, and errands. Without an external place to keep all this information organized, it takes up space in our brain and keeps us in a state of high alert—continually surprised and nagged by our thoughts.

This is when the Sunday Basket comes in. I'm not saying it's a stand-in for medication or therapy, but it's a tool (just like those) that can help you gain back control, even in challenging times. It certainly was for me. Having these systems allowed me to separate my sometimes-overwhelming thoughts and emotions from the tasks at hand. My brain was in overdrive, and I needed a way to quiet it down. I and so many of my clients have found that keeping paper in one spot and having a habit and routine for maintaining it makes everything seem just a little more attainable.

The Sunday Basket helped me do that. Maybe it can help you, as well.

How to Change Your Life

It's a big promise, I know! And I'm not suggesting that having your papers in order will miraculously improve every aspect of your world. But having a sense of outer order can help lead to inner calm . . . if you're ready and willing to take the steps toward equanimity. Here's how I tell my clients they may be ready to implement the sort of lasting change in their lives that the Sunday Basket represents.

Decide You're Ready to Try Something New

In creating change in life, the decision to change is the first step. However, while most people know that they want to change, they are not clear on what the goal or outcome looks like. When you think about wanting to change, what is the issue you are solving? Maybe you are fed up with the piles of paper in your house. Maybe you are done being embarrassed because you missed another payment, forgot another birthday card, or let another policy lapse. Maybe you are ready to feel as though you are running your life, instead of it running you. Whatever the thing you want to change is, investing in the system tells your brain that you're serious about it and that you believe that you will get the benefit of it. You are also coming to terms with a behavior or habit you have that you recognize is not serving you.

Believe It Can Be Done

Before you can commit to making that change, we have to analyze our behavior and see the areas that need improvement. We have to come to terms with the feelings of responsibility, anxiety, and fear we have about our papers. Many people say, "I can't be organized," and that is not true. Organization is a skill anyone can learn, but often we are driven by fear. Ironically, we are both afraid that we cannot be organized and that we can. We fear failure. But we also fear success and what will happen to our mental story if we change and what that will mean for our obligations going forward. Learning organization is a real shift in identity!

Remove Negativity

Our brains are actually wired to think negatively. This is evolutionary, because the negative things in our lives once could have killed us, so we are wired to consider those things. But in our current society, we are able to be proactive. We no longer have to constantly consider every possible danger. We do not face predatory animals on the way to work. Most of us do not need to save enough food in the fall to survive until spring. Our society has modernized enough that many of our emotional triggers really are not emergent concerns anymore.

Retrain Your Brain

In order to continue to be successful and to deal with our emotions and psychology, we need to retrain our brain. The key to retraining our brain is to consciously create a habit by maintaining a routine. It is simple but not easy. The Sunday Basket gives you the skills and the tools to be proactive.

Compartmentalize Your Thoughts

A very real psychological benefit of the Sunday Basket is that we put our papers into an actual place on the kitchen counter. This creates a physical presence for our paper. This helps to establish the habit of putting all the paper together in one place. Having it easily visible helps to trigger the reminder to sort the contents on Sunday. The more thoughts we try to keep in our brains, the less room there is for anything else (such as creative pursuits, daydreaming, or planning for the future). Writing down thoughts and reminders on paper helps to keep your brain clear. The more you use the Sunday Basket, the more your brain will trust that you will go through the notes and act on them.

Set Goals

The act of creating a slash pocket sends the message to our brain that a thought, goal, or project is real and important. Having a dream of reading more books sounds good, but if it is just a thought in your brain, it is likely to be discounted while also adding to your anxiety or stress. Once you have a slash pocket for this topic, you are more likely to look up books you want to read, keep a list, remember to check books out of the library, and make time to read in your schedule.

Build a Habit

The Sunday Basket system takes about six weeks for the average person to build into a routine. In order to be successful with learning this organizational skill, you need to commit to using the Sunday Basket religiously for this introductory period. At first, there will be a deluge of actionable papers, and it may take a long time to get through the Sunday Basket. It also won't always feel as though you are making progress during the first six weeks. However, after using the system for at least that long, life usually happens and Sunday Basket users miss a week. Although I do not recommend it, missing a week of sorting and using your Sunday Basket can be an eye-opening experience to the value you are getting from your Sunday Basket.

Maintain It for Life

Life is ever changing. That is one of the reasons that paper organization can be so complex. Any system works only if it is maintained. Maintenance keeps a system fresh and functional. The same is true for your Sunday Basket. Although you will look at each item or slash pocket in the Sunday Basket every week, I also recommend reviewing all the contents three to four times a year. As I mentioned earlier, I generally divide my year into three segments—the New Year (January through May), Summer (June through August), and the School Year (September through December).

At the transition between each of these three new years, you will want to take a step back and review all the slash pockets in your Sunday Basket system. I often call this a deep dive or a reboot. Stop and really consider if all the slash-pocket topics should stay active during the next 100 to 120 days. Sometimes the reality is that we are not able to actually do all that we want to do. We start out each year with good intentions, but unexpected events happen and we need to revise our plans. Renegotiating dreams or putting some plans on hold is not failure; it is responsible living. It is also important to see if there are new things that should be added to your Sunday Basket. One way to do this is to look ahead on the calendar and see if there are any new slash pockets that you need to add (do you need to plan for spring break, or summer vacation, or a fall sports activity)? And for that we need to take a look at our calendars.

CHAPTER 8

Create Your Calendar

How to Get from To-Do to Done

FACT: Parents spend an average of 23 percent of their free time scheduling and coordinating their children's and family's schedules.

(Harris Interactive, as cited in "Surprising Stats," *Simply Orderly*, http://simplyorderly.com/surprising-statistics)

Claire was one of my first clients. She started off as a blog reader and tried to implement the Sunday Basket method on her own. But no matter how hard she tried, her home was still chaotic. She decided to bite the bullet and pay to have a consultation even though she didn't have the funds. Somehow, she had to be missing something.

She was a girl after my own heart. She loved books, learning, and researching. She was also at a crossroads in her life: she was turning forty, her children were growing up, and she was thinking about what she would do next. Our children were in the similar middle-school-to-high-school age range (and I knew how chaotic family life could be), so we bonded right away.

We got straight to work going through her Sunday Basket, sorting papers into the correct slash pockets. The system was set up well, and Claire was using it weekly, so something else was missing. But I didn't know what it was. I started asking questions.

What are your mornings like? When do you get up? What is your routine? The boys' routines? What do you eat? When do you need to leave the house?

What are your days like? Go through each typical Monday, Tuesday, Wednesday, etc.

When do you get home? What do you eat for dinner? What after-school activities do you have? What about church? Go through each typical Monday evening, Tuesday evening, etc.

It was readily obvious to me that this working-from-home, single, homeschooling mom was flat-out not able to do the current responsibilities on her plate. Not because she wasn't capable. But because she simply didn't have the time.

In addition to running her home solo, this supermom was also homeschooling her kids, schlepping them to various activities (her boys played football on separate teams for a total of twenty hours a week), and trying to fit her own activities and interests into the mix. Plus, their whole family had food sensitivities and intolerances, which meant eating out was not an option.

And while we both intuitively knew this wasn't working, neither of us could pinpoint why. We tried stacking tasks (she did work in the car while the boys were at football), batching tasks (doubling recipes and eating the same food two days in a row), and getting up earlier and staying up late—all to no avail.

Then it hit me! We were not putting *driving time* on her calendar. As soon as we identified when she would be in the car, we immediately saw the problem. Twenty-five hours a week were lost to driving. She immediately started putting all driving on her new Google Calendar and for the first time was able to see where the lost time had gone. Now she had to decide what she could cut to get all her tasks done. She decided to stop homeschooling for one year to get other areas of her life in check. She also started carpooling with another family to gain back some precious hours of travel time.

In the end, Claire was eventually able to make it through this hectic (if wonderful in so many ways) season of her life. And by the end, she'd even carved out a little time for herself as well. And isn't that ultimately a win for each of us?

Properly using a calendar will validate your workload, increase your productivity, and allow you to give yourself grace! So many of us use our calendars only for appointments that involve other people. We miss adding routine tasks and personal to-dos in our calendar blocks. This creates unrealistic expectations on our time and a lack of fulfillment at the end of an exhausting day.

You must figure out where your time is going in order to find more time and prioritize your tasks. The Orange folder in your Sunday Basket holds anything that you need to schedule or put on a calendar. **I want you to really think about your schedule and your life.** Grab a cup of coffee and spend some time thinking about your calendar, what items you need to access, how portable you need to be, and how you like to plan your days.

Put All the Dates from Your Sunday Basket on Your Calendar

A large part of paper management is having a reliable, portable way to keep track of our schedules. This is vital in order to be able to make decisions about agreeing to activities and to planning our time. Calendars still come in two basic varieties: digital and paper.

Digital Calendars

I use a digital calendar because I can access it from my phone on the go and share it with my team and family.

But the real reason I love my digital calendar is because I can add in my to-dos, schedule driving time, and prioritize how I spend my business hours. Now if something comes up, I can look at my calendar and see what task I am deleting or deferring to take advantage of the new opportunity.

My digital calendar didn't start out this way, but over the past five years I have achieved most of my goals and increased productivity through calendar management and planning. Digital calendars give me a greater ability to do this detailed planning.

My digital calendar view default is weekly on my computer and daily on my phone.

PROS	CONS
Portable	Requires battery
Have infinite access to past and future	Limited access for others in event of illness or injury
Can sync across multiple devices (auto backup)	Multiple choices—may not sync with other apps or systems
Easy to change plans	Company access to your data
Unlimited events	
Can sync to outside electronic calendars	
Can share with others	
Most people take phones everywhere	
Can set reminders/alerts	
Can email self your daily schedule	
Multiple views	

Paper (Analog) Calendars

I have been using a paper calendar since high school. I remember taking my babysitting money and poring through the calendar options at Hallmark and OfficeMax.

Paper calendars help me see the big picture of where my time is going. I tend to put only big events on my monthly calendar. The first thing I did over a year before this book was published was grab 2020 and 2021 calendars to map out all the stops I wanted to make over the nine months of my book tour.

Seeing those dates along with holidays, family birthdays, and company initiatives helped me realistically see how many days I could be gone at a time and in a month. I then went back and thought about which areas of the country would be best to visit in each month. Florida and Texas moved to January and February, while Chicago and Cleveland moved up to September to avoid snow.

My favorite default for a paper calendar is a monthly or several-months-at-a-time view.

PROS	CONS
Never needs to charge	Difficult to back up
Research shows writing causes different memory pathways	Can be lost, damaged, or destroyed
Fully customizable	Limited amount of time covered
	Writing space is limited
	Needs to be carried
	Changing plans leaves a mess
	Hard to share calendar

Choose Your Calendar System

Find a calendar system that works for you. Put all the school dates, flyers, doctors' appointments, family birthdays, and holidays on that calendar today. I also like to add in my carpool and driving times on most weeks. This helps me be more realistic about my available times, and I also make sure I do not leave anyone stranded anywhere.

As of the writing of this book, most people are using a hybrid system. Keeping an online master calendar and writing out a daily or weekly plan works for many people. This captures most of the pros of both systems and minimizes the cons. The truly important part of keeping your calendar organized is creating a system that is realistic and simple enough that you use it consistently.

Before electronic calendars, keeping our family calendar updated and accurate used to be a full-time job. I was always adding or removing things from the calendar. Plus, with a physical calendar, if I was out and received an invitation or tried to make an appointment, I had to try to remember my calendar and then remember to keep the little card and add it to the master calendar.

Google Calendar

I personally prefer Google Calendar. If you are an Apple user, iCal is very similar. Google Calendar is a free online calendar system that has an app that can be installed on all cell phones. An entry on any computer, tablet, or phone syncs to all the other devices. I can put different categories of activities in different colors. Google Calendar allows for repeating events (you can repeat an event on the fifteenth of the month, or the second Tuesday of every month, or weekly, or whatever you need). I color-code everything on my calendar. For my current life, I have different colors for Organize 365 team meetings, home-schooling my daughter, errands, time with my spouse, and personal. Additionally, I helped my husband and teenagers create their own Google accounts, and they share their calendars with me. Each of these different calendars can be turned off and on with a click of the mouse to customize my view.

Google Calendar has the ability to view the calendar by day, week, or month. Furthermore, a daily overview of your schedule can be set up to send to yourself by email each morning. The calendar also includes the ability to give reminders prior to and at the start of scheduled activities. It is possible to set reminders for onetime and recurring events. If you need help remembering to take out the trash cans, give your pet a monthly medication, or check your furnace filters, you can set this on the calendar and it shows up until the task is marked complete.

I keep my calendar open as I use my Sunday Basket and plan my week. I can see in advance at a glance which days are packed full. I can also see where I have bigger blocks of open time to work on projects that require more intense concentration.

Here are the reasons I continue to choose my digital calendar:

- *I can have multiple calendars under the same account (work, social, church, activity, etc.).*
- *I can easily add recurring events.*
- *I can color-code events in my own life.*
- *I can color-code my family members.*
- *I can link to calendars for my husband and kids.*
- *I can share my calendar with my team members.*
- *I can set alarms and reminders varying times in advance.*
- *I can have Google send me a morning email with my schedule for the day.*

While my Google Calendar is my master calendar, I also use an analog system. Each evening, I write out an index card with my schedule and my most important tasks and errands for the next day. Setting out my plan for each day in advance allows me to have a sense of my big-picture schedule, and when life throws curveballs, I have the best information available to decide what to delegate, defer, or delete.

The Google Calendar has several different types of data points you can enter:

- **Events.** *Events are placed on days and times. Events can also be set to recur at different intervals. This is best used for scheduled appointments. You can also set a location for an event and your phone may help you to know when to leave in order to be on time.*
- **Reminders.** *Reminders can be onetime or recurring. Reminders can be set ahead of time at any interval prior to the event (you can remind yourself the week before, the day before, thirty minutes before, or even five minutes before). They stay active until the "Mark as done" option is selected. If you set a reminder to give your dog heartworm medicine, it moves from day to day until you tell the calendar you have completed the item.*
- **Tasks.** *Tasks show up on the sidebar and can act as a to-do list. The most recent version of the online calendar allows you to add items to the task list on the sidebar to the right. Tasks can be recurring or can be given due dates.*

Color-Code Your Calendar

I suggest color-coding your calendar. Each of my kids has a color, different types of work in my business have a color, my husband has a color, and I have my own color. Each day and week, I look at my calendar from my computer and can easily see by color if that week is heavy with work or family activities. Seeing my schedule at a glance like this helps me to know if I have work time available or not.

Google Calendar has two different ways to color-code the content. You can create multiple calendars for the same account. With separate calendars, you can toggle them off and on using a checkbox on the left side of a computer screen or under the settings icon on a phone app. This allows you to see different layers of your schedule in varying configurations. This can be helpful if you have multiple family members and your spouse or children are managing their own calendars and you want to be able to view the overall calendar or add family events like parties. Google does offer an option to get a daily email with your calendar contents, but it currently includes only your primary calendar.

Conversely, you can put the items on the same calendar (typically the default calendar associated with the account), but you can assign different color-coding to the items on the calendar. If you choose that option, you cannot typically turn specific colors on and off, so you will always see the whole calendar. With this setup of color-coding, if you elect to get a daily schedule, it will include all the events on your primary calendar for your Google account.

Some of the members of the Organize 365 community also use color-coding to reflect the Sunday Basket colors. So important events would be red. Self would be pink. Family would be blue. Work would be green. And so on.

Plan Your Ideal Week

Start with a blank week, and think about what a perfect week (with no unexpected events) would look like for you and your family. When do you do your best work? What things do you want to include for yourself (gym, hair, rest, reading, etc.)? When will you do housework? How much time do you need to prepare food? When do you like to go grocery shopping? How much time do you need to spend driving around?

See if you can schedule a block of time to take care of errands and interruptions for the week. Consider if you can hire help if you need it. At different times in my life, I have hired a personal assistant, I have had a house cleaner, and I have outsourced my laundry to the folks at the Laundromat.

As you work through your Sunday Basket and your calendar, be honest with yourself about your life and your schedule. Are there events on your calendar that you dread? Do you attend an event or class that leaves you drained? Get rid of things that do not line up with your phase of life and your purpose. We cannot go through life and just keep adding things to our workload and our calendar. Declutter. Make some margin to allow new things to enter your life.

Schedule Your Week

Look over your calendar and consider all the things that have already been put on it. Then fill in other things you must do that week. For our family, drive time to school and a lot of doctors' appointments fill my calendar. For you, it might be soccer tournaments, or dance practice, or getting ready for a spelling bee.

As you work through your Sunday Basket, you will want to make an appointment with yourself to complete your most important tasks. You may want to set aside an hour to make your phone calls. You can see where you may have a large enough block of time to complete your errands.

Think about your schedule. See which tasks are similar and can be batched together. You may find it easier to have a single errand day and run all over town, rather than having to go to a different store every night after work. Look at how your days flow. Does your time help you to accomplish the most important things? Or are you too busy just racing around like a rat in a wheel? Is everything in your calendar in the best place to complete the task? For example, if you do your best thinking and focus at work in the morning, do not make that your email or housecleaning time. Save those things for the times when your brain is less effective.

If you are always running late, do not seem to have enough time in the day, or stress out about getting everyone where they need to be, I suggest putting *all* your driving hours on your calendar for at least six weeks. Physically seeing that time as busy will help you stop trying to squeeze "one more thing" onto your calendar.

I do my best to separate my work time from my family time. I have been a mom who works from home for over a decade. As my children have gotten older, I have found it beneficial to be more clear-cut with separating my family time from my work.

I also try to schedule time for myself. I have been working on ensuring that I schedule date nights with my husband, once-a-month outings with my girlfriends, and a haircut every six weeks.

Each Sunday, as I go through my Sunday Basket, I think

about each role I play in my life and try to make sure my to-do list and calendar have all the information to be successful for the week. Here are some of the questions I used (and still use) to plan my week:

- *Is anyone traveling this week?*
- *When are the adults working this week?*
- *What do the kids need this week?*
- *How are the kids getting to and from each calendar event? (Who is driving?)*
- *What is our dinner plan?*
- *Does anyone need lunch money?*
- *Does anyone need to bring along a snack or meal?*
- *Does anyone need special clothing (sports uniform, gym clothes, Scout uniform)?*
- *Does anyone need anything for a project?*
- *Does anyone need to bring a gift?*
- *Do I need to run any errands this week?*
- *Am I planning to work on any home projects this week?*
- *Do we have any family activities planned?*
- *Have I planned anything fun for the family lately?*
- *Can we fit in some fun this week?*

This is meant to be not an exhaustive list but more of a brainstorming list for your own planning for the week. As you learn what kinds of questions you need to consider in setting up your week, it can be helpful to make a list and keep it in your Sunday Basket to help with your planning. The most important thing to realize is that *time is finite.* You are limited in how much you can cram into a week. I highly recommend that if you are in charge of driving others around, you include that time on your calendar. It will help you have a more realistic understanding of how much time you have in a given week. In order to be successful in actually completing your to-do items each week, do not try to schedule your maximum output for a near-perfect week. Allow lots of time and margin, and you can always add additional things if you have free time later in the week. And if something comes up, you are not grossly overcommitted.

And, of course, add your Sunday Basket time to your weekly calendar. In general, I recommend starting with 90 to 120 minutes per week to spend working through your Sunday Basket. In reality, it takes me all day Sunday to get ready for the week. In addition to going through my Sunday Basket, I pay bills, change the sheets, do six loads of laundry, clean the house, refill the weekly medicine dispensers, and plan carpools and other transportation. In my family, my husband does the grocery shopping, but if I were responsible for meal planning and grocery shopping, that would go on my calendar, as well.

Look over your calendar and the plan for the week. Try to find a larger chunk of time, ideally four hours or more, but at least two hours. Use these blocks of time to work on important tasks for the week and to move toward your goals. These can be excellent time blocks to focus on your paper organization and to make progress getting organized.

The frustrating reality is that we generally have the time, energy, and focus to complete only one to three tasks a day *total*. This does not mean we make the bed, brush our teeth, and make dinner and call it a day. It *does* mean that you can focus on only a few things outside of your normal routines. That is not failure—that is life! And when I list one to three things, that includes *both* work and home projects. You cannot expect to double that and finish six items! Underplan and overdeliver!

Plan for the Unexpected

Planning is the best way to increase your productivity. For each minute you spend planning your week, you will save three to five minutes in the upcoming week. Optimizing your morning and evening routines will help shave off time from daily tasks and allow you more free time to focus on living your life with purpose. You will become productive and fulfilled. As you embrace what you are uniquely created to do, you will inspire others to live their life with purpose and fulfillment.

I am super organized. I am uber-productive. And I schedule everything. But I cannot control the weather. Several years ago, we had a super cold winter. From January to March, my children never went to school five days out of any week. By April, I was ready to lose it.

Over time, I have learned to allow margin in my weekly planning. I really plan only about three tasks to complete each day. Some tasks are larger than others, and I try to balance my workload. For example, scheduling a doctor's appointment would take less time and energy than cleaning out a kid's closet. I try to balance small wins and large tasks so that I make progress each day.

No matter what, you will not always follow your plan. People get sick. Pets get sick. Cars break down. Accidents happen. But when you start your week with a plan and you know you are doing your best to finish, you can adjust when life throws you curveballs.

We spend a lot of time trying to find the perfect calendar or make the perfect binder and then wonder why they do not "work" for us. It is the *act* of planning that makes the calendar and Sunday Basket *work*. Calendars and Sunday Baskets hold information. When we plan our week this way, we move toward *action* and *accountability*.

Planning your week is where that elusive productivity we all strive for originates. Remember to give yourself grace and try different time-saving ideas as you go. What works for one family will not work for the next. Don't worry what everyone else is doing; figure out what works for you!

Part III

ditch the filing cabinet

CHAPTER 9

The Binder Solution

Why the Best Storage Is Portable

FACT: Email is actually *increasing* print volume by 40 percent.

(*Document Magazine*, as cited in Sherry Borsheim, "Organizing & Time Management Statistics," *Simply Productive*, March 12, 2012, https://www.simplyproductive.com/2012/03/time-management-statistics/)

In the fall of 2017, I sat helplessly refreshing my Facebook news feed. Bouncing from Twitter for the latest news, to the Weather Channel for flood predictions, to Facebook for news was a full-time job. Hurricane Harvey was followed by Hurricane Irma and then Hurricane Maria, and I grew increasingly concerned for all my friends, my clients, and their families in the region. I saw their real-time updates as they moved all their important possessions, pets, and people into attics, with hatchets to break through the roof for potential rescue. The sheer amount of water being dumped on Texas was of biblical proportions.

And then came the California fires. Sixty-one total fires in

2017 alone. So many homes and lives destroyed. As my business has grown and my contacts have spread across North America and the world, barely a month goes by when someone in my network isn't affected by a natural disaster of some sort. The questions I get in this situation are always the same: "Lisa, what can we do to get organized for the evacuation?"

Those natural disasters (and the many, many that have followed) made me realize: we must ditch the filing cabinet, once and for all. When homeowners need to leave quickly, they can't waste precious time digging through years of paper to find the few valuable documents that are essential to take with them. What good is a filing system that isn't portable and accessible in times of great need?

My Issue with Filing Cabinets

Once you have done your initial purge and you have your Sunday Basket up and running, it is a good time to deal with any remaining files and paper piles you have not yet organized. It's time to create your binders.

Grab a pile or file and open it up. Plop it all on the floor or your designated sorting table. Before you go forward in the process, *purge again*. By now, you'll be familiar with the sorts of paper that can go—and I'll bet you find lots more that is redundant, unnecessary, and ready to be recycled or shredded. Everything left will end up in your Sunday Basket (rare), a reference binder (most), or your archive system (rare).

And none of them will end up in a filing cabinet if I have anything to say about it!

I stopped talking about files a few years ago, and I no longer think you should have a filing cabinet at all. They are not portable. The majority of what you put into a filing cabinet you will never reference again. And, worst of all, they put no limit on the amount of paper you can keep.

Earlier in the book, I talked about the generational mind-set differences. Our parents and grandparents (and some of us!) needed to hang on to lots of paper. But that's not the case any longer. Our filing cabinets are holding us back and keeping us from optimum organization. Here's why.

First, filing cabinets are rarely in the heart of the home. They are far away from where we live day to day, and it takes a highly disciplined person to gather up the mail and other incoming papers, sort, and then file correctly far away from the bustle of family life. If you have young children who need to be watched, it is even more difficult. Most people resort to dumping to-be-filed papers on top of the filing cabinet and walking away.

Second, filing cabinets require specific parts to function correctly. Filing cabinets were designed for office environments and often have a hanging rack, hanging file folders, and manila folders inside of the hanging file folders. If you add a new file to the system, you need to add at least two additional parts, and you need somewhere to store all your extra supplies.

Third, in order to be effective, we need to remember how we filed a particular piece of paper in order to retrieve it and file the updated copy. For example, you may file a piece of paper for your car under: auto, car, vehicle, or the brand name of the car. If your system is alphabetical, you would have to look in all four (or more) of the possible places for the correct file. If you have a house where two adults share the filing system, it gets even more complicated.

In terms of organizing household papers, there has been nothing significantly new on the market in eighty years. We are still using paper-organization and storage systems that our grandmothers learned either in home economics classes or in the workplace. I want to introduce you to a system that works for homes and families in our current day and age. Rather than using old-fashioned filing cabinets, the answer is your Sunday Basket for active papers and basic reference binders for your reference/basic archive papers. These simple, portable systems can live in your kitchen. And they're designed to work for you, your family, your home, your lifestyle, and your paper.

How to Create Your Own Binders

When you begin to organize your papers, the Sunday Basket should come first. Your active day-to-day papers must be under control. If you are not able to track and pay your electric bill on time, it does not matter if you have pretty binders full of your household manuals. Establish your Sunday Basket routine first, and I recommend about six weeks of consistent use before you start to create your binders. In the next chapters, I will walk you through the same organizing steps to dealing with reference papers by building specific binders.

Binders are portable and give you a constraint of space. I limit myself to two-inch binders and make sure each has a specific purpose. The limits of the binder force you to purge and keep your papers current. For example, I have one financial binder, which holds *all* the financial documents from our entire house. There are no financial papers anywhere else. It prevents us from keeping the expired homeowners' insurance policy from eight years ago. When the new policy arrives, I pay the bill and put the new paperwork inside the binder. I remove the old paperwork and recycle or shred it, and my papers stay organized, useful, portable, and profitable.

The organization inside your binder can and should be customized. In the following chapters I will share with you how the Organize 365 binders are set up. Each binder is divided into five sections. I prefer a set of five slash pockets to divide those sections because they are easy to see and can hold papers you have not yet had a chance to three-hole punch or put in sheet protectors. This keeps your binders more up-to-date and organized.

Binders ensure that your useful reference paper is easy to access, easy to update, and easy to move (if you were to move to a new home or evacuate for an emergency).

Discard Useless Papers

When exploring your older saved papers, begin your organizing as we did the Sunday Basket system—with decluttering. Hopefully you got rid of some of this backlog in the Big Purge, but now that you're more comfortable with this process, you'll proceed faster and more boldly. Carefully evaluate if you need to keep the paper at all. In all my years of professionally organizing for homeowners and business owners, the reality is that 85 percent of paper can be safely discarded. The less paper you keep, the easier it will be to organize. As before, paper that can be discarded can be either recycled or shredded. Remember: Shred only those things with private, personally identifying information on them. Recycle as much as possible of the other paper.

Decluttering can be such a challenge. Much like the physical clutter in our homes, a great deal of the paper we save is "aspiration clutter"—representing the lives we dream of having, not the ones we're currently living. As you go through your old files, you will find old budgets, school notes from years ago, and old medical bills that may remind you of happy or sad times (a new baby or a cancer diagnosis). Really think about whether you need this material in the future or whether it represents some aspect of your past that you can leave behind without regret.

Divide Papers into Categories

I think the best solution for our reference papers is in a binder. When I refer to reference papers, I am speaking of papers we need only a few times a year or will need to access information in an emergency. This does not mean that we should take our two to four filing cabinets full of hanging files and stick all that paper into binders. No one can load four file drawers' worth of paper into a car when evacuating or rushing to the hospital.

There are four main types of binders that are needed to organize all the paper for an entire household.

1. **Household Reference Binder.** This binder focuses on all the paperwork that is needed when owning a house. It holds a record of all the decorating decisions we make in

our home, including light fixtures, paint colors, flooring information, and similar items. It holds a list of all the home improvements we have completed, along with purchase and warranty information (roof, window replacements, siding, etc.). It can also hold outdoor information for lawn, yard, and landscaping. You can include instructions for infrequently completed but detailed tasks, like programming the thermostat or winterizing the sprinkler system. Finally, appliance manuals, receipts, and warranty information are all stored in this binder. The binder is actually meant to be left out for prospective buyers when we sell our homes and left as a reference to stay with the building.

2. Financial Organizing Binder. This binder can serve one of two purposes. First, if we create it for our own home and family, it is a reference in the event that someone needs to help with our financial paperwork during a time of injury or illness. In many families, one person knows how the bills get paid and where the bank accounts are housed. This binder provides one place to keep financial, auto, insurance, and retirement paperwork. The second use for this binder is when acting as a power of attorney or as an executor of an estate for a loved one. I initially designed this binder based on what I needed when I was in charge of settling my late father's estate.

3. Medical Organizing Binder. This binder holds all the medical information for a single person. In my family, my kids both have medical needs with several healthcare providers. I have a medical binder for each child that I have used to keep documents and records and to hold medical records. For my children, it was super important to keep track of medications and treatments we tried that did not work. I also keep records of vital signs and information discussed at doctors' visits.

4. Household Operations Binder. This binder I think of like the lesson plan for the home. It is a place to record family holiday and celebration traditions. It is the playbook a babysitter, pet sitter, or other household help would use to take care of the daily needs of your family. It includes meal-planning pages and party-planning pages. It is a single place to record where those infrequently used items are stored or how to best arrange the holiday decorations.

5. BONUS: School Memory Binder. This binder can be made for each child in your family, and when you have time for additional archive papers, it can be fun to make one for you and one for your spouse. This binder will generally hold school art, awards, and memories in chronological order. You can simply slip the items into page protectors. Large projects can be captured in photos, both of the project alone and of the student with the project.

6. BONUS: IEP Binder. If you are the parent of a child who needs special education services or who has an Individual Education Program (IEP), chapter 15 will walk you through how to organize all your paperwork and improve your ability to advocate for your child.

As you begin to slog through and sort your paper backlog, it can be a big time-saver to sort directly into binder categories. Rather than getting sidetracked by trying to stop and put each individual piece of paper into a binder as you go along, I recommend getting a bankers' box for each binder topic. As you run across papers that are worth putting into binders, just toss them into the appropriate container. Then, when you have a block of time to build and fill out your binder, you can work on a single binder at a time. Furthermore, if you *do* need to find a reference paper before your binder is assembled, you'll have to sort through only a limited stack.

These four basic binders will house the majority of your paperwork. The goal is to have only a few binders of essential papers. Adding more binders adds complexity to the simple system you are striving for. If you do decide to add on extra binders to this system, make sure your binder has a clear *purpose*. Do not allow a binder to become a catchall or a dumping ground for delayed decisions; those belong in the Sunday Basket until you take action or delete the idea.

Reference Your Binders

As you move your papers out of dusty old filing cabinets stuffed with what is likely trash, you will find that you can increase your productivity. First, having your paperwork in simple-to-grab groups makes it easy to complete your Sunday Basket to-do items. Do you need your driver's license number and insurance policy number for your renewal? Grab your Financial Organizing Binder and fill out the form. Wondering when you had your last annual physical? Grab your Medical Organizing Binder, look it up, and call to make an appointment. A friend asks for a referral for a pest control service? Grab your Household Operations Binder and send the information right over. When your washing machine breaks down, you can grab your Household Reference Binder, get the model number, purchase date, and warranty information in a minute to schedule a service call.

Maintenance

The trick to making binders useful is regular maintenance. As your new homeowners' insurance policy comes in, replace the old one. As you plan for a holiday dinner this year, keep a copy of the menu and your favorite recipes together (that will help with next year's grocery list). When you buy a new TV, put the manual and receipt in a page protector, and recycle the old manual and TV.

How Do I Decide Which Binder to Complete First?

If you have an immediate need in your life right now, start with the binder that focuses on your highest priority. If you do not have an immediate need that warrants your completing a binder, I suggest you create your binders in this order:

A NOTE ABOUT BINDERS

As a professional organizer, teacher, and productivity specialist, I have some strong opinions about binders. To be blunt, I am a total binder snob. When you move out of filing cabinets, you will want a quality product to house your important papers. Many of these binders will be frequently referenced, and you want to enjoy using them.

Here are the optimal binder specifications you are looking for: a deluxe D-ring two-inch binder with an extended cover. A deluxe binder is made with a thicker cardboard and thicker plastic coating, and will stand up to the regular use you will give this binder over the next twenty years. A few dollars more will make all the difference five years from now as your binder protects the hundreds of papers you put in each one. Most deluxe binders will have a D ring. This will help your papers lie flat in the binder and be easier to flip through as you search deeper in the binder's pages. Binders come in all sizes, from a half inch to five inches thick. The two-inch binder is the sweet spot for your home organization binders.

The last consideration is to find a binder that has an extended cover. That extra half inch will protect your slash pocket tabs that you will use to divide the contents of your binder. I am often adding slash pockets from my Sunday Basket into my binders at different times of the year, especially in my Home Operations Binder. Our annual trip to the beach has a slash pocket that I put in my Sunday Basket when I book the plane tickets. From that time until our trip, I add notes, receipts, and reading material I want to take with me. Then when our trip is over, the slash pocket goes back in the Home Operations Binder until next spring.

1. Household Reference
- *Do this first if you are planning to move or sell your home.*

2. Financial
- *Do this first if you are in charge of an estate or a loved one's finances.*

3. Medical (one binder per person in the home)
- *Do this first if you are a caretaker for another person or have personal significant health challenges.*

4. Household Operations
- *Do this first if you are big on traditions and family celebrations.*

BONUS (if needed)

1. School Memory
- *This is a place to store the writing, art, certificates, and memories from school.*

2. IEP
- *This is a specific binder (in addition to the Medical Organizing Binder) to help organize the paperwork that comes with having a child who has special school needs and an IEP.*

Where Should I Store My Binders?

Many of my clients tell me that their binders have been a lifesaver in all different kinds of life crises and emergencies. People have been able to take their binders when evacuating from wildfires. Other people loaded up binders when they were leaving flooding areas after hurricanes. Others have taken the binders across the country when caring for a loved one to ensure that their own home and life could be cared for remotely.

When you decide where in your home to store your binders, there are several things to consider. First, how many binders do you have? Second, how is your home currently structured? Consider where you most often enter and exit your home. Do you have non–family members who come in and out, like cleaning people or dog walkers? (If so, do you want to store the binders in a less central or more secure location?) Then, think about how likely you are to need to evacuate or depart in a hurry. How frequently do weather events or natural disasters occur in your part of the world? Think about your family. How many adults help out with the paperwork? Who might need to access the information in your binder? Also, consider how often you reference different types of information. Personally, I prioritize ease of access over hiding my binders away.

It is not failure to try different locations in your home. Sometimes, you may benefit from keeping all the binders together, and other times you may find it works better if you separate them by topic or room. In general, a thief is not going to look through your binder collection when looking for valuables. However, you may want to keep a digital copy of the contents, and even a physical copy of your most important documents (birth certificate, marriage certificate, etc.) in a fireproof safe or safe-deposit box.

Here are some places you may want to consider:

- *On your kitchen counter near your Sunday Basket*
- *In a kitchen cabinet*

- *In the mudroom or entryway*
- *With recipe books in the kitchen*
- *With photo albums*
- *On a shelf in the office*
- *In your craft area*

Feel free to put a false label on the edge, such as "Science Notes" or "Appliance Manuals," that would be uninteresting to a potential thief. Most of the time, if you keep a binder "hidden" in plain sight in a place it would reasonably belong, you will be safe. However, if you try to hide it somewhere it looks out of place, like in a refrigerator or in a linen closet, it will be more conspicuous.

The Real Benefit of Binders

The benefit of binders is the sense of security you'll have, knowing that you know where your most important papers are—and that you can take them with you if you need to leave in a hurry. I heard from so many members of my online community in fall of 2018, when the camp fires were raging in California and Hurricane Florence was coming ashore in the Carolinas. So many of them checked in to tell me that they were safely on the road, evacuating with family, pets, and organized binders in their cars.

One woman named Lauren shared her story with me: "While we are so fortunate not to have flooding at my house, my neighborhood and town still are dealing with flooded streets. When the hurricane was coming, our family evacuated and I took my binders with me. I can't tell you how my Sunday Basket and binders have saved me during all of this. When my banking website was down and I couldn't pay bills, I pulled out my Household Operations Binder and was able to call to make payments with all my information at hand or go to the individual creditor sites. We were able to make it into my daughter's doctor appointment, and I had all her information, chargers, and supplies safe. This system has truly been a lifesaver. Now my priority is getting my binders and important docs, photos, and scrapbooks scanned to the cloud."

And that's what we're all looking for, isn't it? A little peace of mind.

CHAPTER 10

Your Household Reference Binder

How to Organize the Papers for Your Physical Home

FACT: More than 40 percent of printouts are discarded within twenty-four hours.

(Daniel Lyons, "Why Xerox Is Helping Customers Use Less Paper," *Newsweek*, November 20, 2008, https://www.newsweek.com/why-xerox -helping-customer-use-less-paper-84783)

Selling your home is an all-consuming task. Emily was overwhelmed preparing for her real estate agent, knowing that all her paper related to house repairs, paint colors, and various home purchases were somewhere in her filing cabinet. She set out to create a Household Reference Binder to sell the house and give the necessary documents to the new owner.

She added value to the household listing by finding and organizing the paper trail of receipts that chronicled all the projects and updates she and her husband had made on their home. She was able to include the related business cards of the repair people they had used for each project. As the binder came together, she was amazed how many of these improvements and repairs she had forgotten about.

Emily also found the original termite inspection with a map of where the baits were around the house. She didn't like remembering this experience. She was worried the termites would hurt the sale of her home. Even so, she felt more in control when she contacted a new termite company and was able to produce the paper they needed to locate the previous baits. She felt so accomplished in that moment and knew she saved her family money with that piece of paper.

The icing on the cake were the household paint colors. Emily's real estate agent loved that she had found the paint chips they used in each room. The real estate agent knew rooms usually need to be completely repainted even if you know the last color that was used, since paint ages on the wall and new paint is sometimes formulated differently, but new homeowners don't know that. One of the top questions buyers ask after they know they want the house is what colors the rooms are painted. Having this information before the house was listed gave the real estate agent confidence: she would have the answers she needed when the showings started.

As Millennials move into adulthood, they account for 68 percent of all first-time homebuyers and more than 32 percent of the US housing market in total.[1] Maintaining a simple and duplicative record-keeping system is imperative for all generations.

Baby Boomers are considering downsizing their homes, and current buyers are more educated about home ownership than ever before. There are many home improvement and home buying shows in the current media. Homebuyers want to know about home maintenance records and home improvements that have been completed, and many adults are looking for lower levels of yard work and house needs. A Household Reference Binder takes the paperwork that previously languished in the filing cabinet and it puts it all at the fingertips of prospective buyers.

Using Your Household Reference Binder

Each binder is set up in the same order, making it easy to update with relevant information and also to see what papers or documentation you are missing. If you own rentals or a second property, then you can create a binder for each. Having the organized paperwork at your fingertips is so important as you take care of your home.

Personally, I consult my Household Reference Binder two or three times a month. The U.S. Bureau of Labor Statistics reports that adults spend between ten and thirty minutes per day on house maintenance, repair, decoration, lawn, and garden tasks.[2] Furthermore, home ownership is expensive. Your Household Reference Binder allows you to record paint colors, home improvements, and repairs.

One of the best uses I have found for my binder is to have the information for my house at my fingertips when things break. All homeowners know that a home *always* has something that breaks, wears out, or needs repair. We have lived in our house more than twenty years. We have repainted the entire outside of our wood house twice, which takes a lot of time and money. We have replaced our skylights twice. We have replaced all the windows and the doors. I cannot even count how many times we have repainted the inside walls. We have recarpeted the floors. We have gutted and renovated the kitchen and the basement. Our kids' rooms have been redecorated five or six times each. And we are now starting to replace the furniture we bought when we first moved in the house. Replacing all the light fixtures is also on the list of improvements we want to do. That is a *lot* of paperwork. But when we do finally go to sell, we can hand the new homeowners the Household Reference Binder, and they will know where to get a replacement globe for the light or which color to use to match some touch-up paint.

My Household Reference Binder has helped to make decisions about when it was worthwhile to repair items and when I was better off just replacing them. When our washer and dryer started to act up, I pulled out my binder and looked at the appliance section. I was able to quickly establish when we had purchased them and how much we had paid. It made the decision to replace the washer instead of repair it an easy one. But I used the same information and was able to determine it made more sense to repair the refrigerator rather than replacing it, even though I really wanted a new one. My binder also helps me know how many bags of mulch we need for our landscaping from year to year. I keep a reminder in there to call the local Boy Scouts, who sell the mulch and are willing to spread it for $1 a bag.

Using Your Household Reference Binder to Sell Your Home

I have no plans to move anytime soon. Unfortunately, the sale of my father's house was not planned. No one plans to sell their childhood home, but most of us one day will, along with planning a funeral and settling an estate. Thirty-five years of paint cans, wallpaper samples, manuals, home repairs, property tax paperwork, and so much more were gathered inside my father's home when he died. It was . . . a lot.

Imagine purchasing a home and receiving all the documentation you need in an organized binder instead of a pile of paint cans, wallpaper rolls, manuals, and files. Many real estate agents are discovering the same thing, which is why the Household Reference Binder is quickly becoming their gift of choice to new homeowners.

Every time my sister and I found an item or piece of paperwork for the new homeowner, we added it to the pile. As we prepared to list the home, we created a Household Reference Binder that organized all the information about the house for our prospective buyers. The more information you can provide, the more likely you are to sell quickly and at an ideal price. Buyers will want to know when the roof was last repaired or replaced. Many will want to know how old appliances and HVAC equipment is. You can also include a plat survey or information about a homeowners association.

Why *You* Need a Household Reference Binder

I'm here to tell you: once you go through the experience of selling your family home, you will come home and purge your

Eliminate more of your paperwork by taking the important information and transferring it to a centralized document. The five-page home improvement tracker (a sample is on the next page) is a great place to start in your Household Reference Binder. In this case, you *will* need to keep the papers related to these improvements to give to the new homeowners when you sell your home, but this synopsis sheet will help you see what you have done to maintain your home and get the best price when you sell.

Find a blank version of this form in the Appendix, or download it at https://organize365.com/paperbook printables.

own house, chanting, "I am *not* going to leave a mess like that for my kids." Remember (and I can't emphasize this enough), you do not need 85 percent of the paper you have saved. Seriously, will you ever need the instruction manual for something like your alarm clock or your iron? If you really do need to figure something out, most of the answers (and even copies of those manuals) can be found online. In the case of your home, you do not need the paint cans, household manuals, or boxes for your electronics, either.

As you are eliminating your filing cabinets, the *best* way to organize this paperwork is into a Household Reference Binder. What you *do* need are the serial numbers, model numbers, purchase prices, and paint colors (name, lot number, or formula). Gathering and organizing this information in a Household

home improvement tracker

Record the year, project details, contractors involved,
and cost of renovations. Use page protectors to store quotes,
permits, receipts, etc., for each project.

Alarm System

Date	Description

Bathrooms

Date	Description

Drywall/Paneling/Paint

Date	Description

Electrical

Date	Description

Reference Binder puts all the paperwork you need in a single book where you can keep everything at your fingertips. The binder will hold all the paperwork that belongs to the structure of the home from one property line to another. This will include all the information you accumulate about the landscaping, the exterior (roof, bricks, siding, windows), and the interior (design elements, appliance purchase and warranty information, and maintenance information). I created my first binder over fifteen years ago and have been refining it since. It changes as our home changes, and I do clean it out regularly. There is no need to keep the manual for the old dishwasher after I buy a new one.

Here is my secret for getting this binder put together and maintained: think of your house as a person. I know, it sounds super weird. But once you change your mind-set, it will really help you going forward. All the things we think about for ourselves, our spouse, our kids, or our pets, like food, clothing, and health maintenance, also need to be done for our house. This binder will help you keep all the information you need to take care of your house just like you take care of your family members.

Let me get a little more concrete. You have a home you need to take care of, and there are certain things you need to do as the home's caretaker. You need to keep the information for your home purchase and/or build. The appliances need to be tracked and maintained and may need new parts like filters or bulbs. You may have electronics that have operation manuals or warranties. You may need to touch up paint or replace some window coverings and will need the information from your original purchase. You need to take care of the outside of the physical house, and you may have landscaping that needs to be cared for. This outside work can include washing windows, trimming bushes, turning outside water on and off, putting up seasonal yard decorations, adding mulch to flower beds, and more. Your home has parts that need to be maintained, serviced, and replaced. Any paperwork about your house that is in a filing cabinet should be purged and then can be used to create your binder.

Again, I will be brutally honest with you. I do not keep my manuals for electronics. I keep the model number and the receipt and ask the internet if I need to figure out how to work or fix something. Oftentimes I keep only the front page of the manual so that I have the model information. I also do not keep even the receipt or manual cover for items that are less than $100 or that I would replace (not repair) if they broke. You do not have to be like me. But maybe try it for something easy like a toaster or an iron and see how it feels to have less paper clutter. This is how I help people eliminate 85 percent of their paper clutter.

The Organize 365 Household Reference Binder

The Household Reference Binder is one of the easiest binders to set up, so I often recommend that people start by creating this binder when they organize their papers.

Your binder will be a combination of saved paperwork and notes. This is the key. Much of the paperwork you have only

PAPERS TO GATHER

- Appliance inventory
- Change of address checklist
- Electronics inventory
- Exterior tracker
- Landscaping tracker
- Homebuyer checklist
- Home décor tracker
- Home furnishings tracker
- Home improvement tracker
- Homeowners association information
- Home seller checklist
- Purchase information
- Rental information
- Yard equipment information

includes one to three pieces of needed information, a model number, price, sale date, and warrantee page; the rest of the manual or document is not needed. So grab a pack of grade-school filler paper with holes and be ready to write down information you want to save, and recycle/shred more paper.

I have included a printable for you to use as a guide as you set up your binder. This is the basic outline of what is included in the Organize 365 binders we use with clients to get all their documentation into one two-inch binder. Feel free to change the contents of your slash pockets based on if you rent or own your home. A home in the city will have different papers than a home on several acres in the country. If you live outside the US, you may have different types of home paperwork. You may modify your categories of paper depending on whether your home is an apartment, a condo, or a house. That is the beauty of binders. I want you to customize each paper storage for *your* life and home.

Purpose: The Household Reference Binder is the place to store all the important documents for your home in one easy-to-access binder. The binder should be used to keep track of reference information about your home.

Create Your Household Reference Binder

Here are the slash-pocket categories you will want to include in your Household Reference Binder:

- *Service Providers*
  - *Window washer*
  - *Tree trimmer*
  - *Landscaper*
  - *Pest control*

- *Home Purchase and Improvements*
  - *Builder information*
  - *Purchase information*
  - *Mortgage information*
  - *Plat survey*

- *Copy of any sales documents*
- *Any homeowners association information*
- *Documents pertaining to any home improvements or upgrades*

- *Home appliances*
  - *Purchase information*
  - *Warranty information*
  - *Manuals*

- *Electronics*
  - *Purchase information*
  - *Warranty information*
  - *Manuals*
  - *Part numbers for replacement parts*

- *Furniture and décor*
  - *Home furnishings*
  - *Décor information (paint formula, fabric swatch, measurements)*
  - *Landscape*
  - *Exterior of home (roof, siding, windows, gutters, etc.)*
  - *Landscape information (plants, plans, care information)*
  - *Yard equipment, tools, and machines*

When you are building your binder, focus on the information you would want to receive if you were purchasing the house or what you would leave behind if you were selling it. Don't worry about removing personal information (like credit card numbers) until you are actually selling your home. If you really do not need the information, you can get rid of it. Remember that at any time you can decide a paper you have saved has served its purpose and you can discard it.

My Household Reference Binder has saved me so much time and money as a homeowner. I am more confident in my home repair decisions knowing that I had all the relevant information when I made my repair or purchasing decision. Your home is your biggest financial investment. Now it is time to take a look at the rest of your financial papers.

CHAPTER 11

Your Financial Organizing Binder

How to Organize Past, Present, and Future Monies

FACT: 23 percent of adults say they pay bills late (and incur fees) because they lose them.

(Harris Interactive, as cited in Joshua Becker, "The Statistics of Clutter," *Becoming Minimalist*, https://www.becomingminimalist.com/the-statistics -of-clutter)

My client Cheryl's husband's passing was unexpected and quick, just a few weeks after his diagnosis. He was her whole world. Nothing seemed the same without him. For their whole marriage, he had handled all the money. Everything about the finances was paralyzing. He had left her notes of what to do and immaculate records of all his investments, multiple bank accounts, and financial records. It was all there.

That was the problem. It was *all* there.

Eighty binders with every single stock report or investment statement in chronological order for the past forty years, many with his handwritten notes about how each stock inside the mutual fund had done month over month. The sheer volume of paper was overwhelming. Where should she start? How much should she keep? What did she need?

In this particular case we spent six sessions spread one month apart to systematically go through the six file drawers and eighty binders, one at a time, shredding 95 percent and putting what was left into three binders. One for monthly bills, one for investments, and one for insurances.

It wasn't until month three that we realized we had been treating two investment accounts (both with close to $50,000 in them) as *one*. We weren't 100 percent sure both brokerage accounts were open and where this extra account could have come from. We were already tracking five accounts with monthly paper statements, but I was pretty sure there was another account that had never merged or been closed based on the binders we continued to comb through.

The next month my client asked me to get on the phone with her as she called the bank. Sure enough, there was another account. It was separate from the main accounts, and the bank hadn't realized it was connected either when my client consolidated all her other holdings. I was floored. Almost $50,000 would have been lost for good in all that paper.

Fifty percent of my professional organization clients were widowed or divorced. Financial papers made them sweat and squirm. Not because they did not have enough money. They all did. The issue was that they did not understand the papers, know what to keep, or have a way to organize them.

As the executor of an estate, there are many hats you don

simultaneously, and often in the blink of an eye. Few are prepared for this important role. And although we all know that we are going to pass at some point, few of us have prepared our paperwork and wishes for those who will be in charge of managing them. All of a sudden, we are tasked with planning the funeral, selling the family home, and handling the other assets and expenses of the estate. All too often we are also caring for our own home and our immediate families, and we may be working for income as well.

Unfortunately, time will not stand still, and your regular life responsibilities will march on through this tough time. With the Financial Organizing Binder by your side, you will be able to search for the relevant information and settle the estate with confidence. The Financial Organizing Binder is designed to help you find all the account numbers, contacts, and relevant information you and your lawyer need to settle the estate after you go back home. No matter what generation you are part of, life is unpredictable. Unfortunately, loss can come at any time. The Financial Organizing Binder is useful in the day-to-day and to establish records for the person in charge of your estate.

Using Your Financial Organizing Binder

Financial paperwork is thick and intimidating. Remember that pack of filler paper I had you use while making the Home Reference Binder? You will need that again here. The essential piece of the Financial Organizing Binder is knowing where your money is, who is managing it, what your account number is, and how to get hold of that company. This chapter will get you started in completing this puzzle.

It took most of a year for me to finalize my father's estate, and creating this binder was invaluable. We needed to clear all the contents out of his home, close up accounts, and collect life insurance policies. The law requires you to file a final personal income tax return for the deceased person, and you may need to file an income tax return for the estate as well.

I created the Financial Organizing Binder with one thing in mind: supporting someone settling an estate. One tip: in most cases, finding the financial documents themselves is easier than finding the information *on* the documents. I suggest you have a highlighter or two handy as we dive into your financial paper piles.

Organizing my own family's finances into a single binder seemed like a mammoth task at first. I emptied our filing cabinet and sorted everything into piles. I decided what I needed to keep and what needed to be shredded or recycled. I then sorted my papers into the areas listed on pages 199–200. As you sort, highlight names, expiration or maturation dates, the date of this paper's printing, and account numbers. This will help you as you sort three different investments with the same parent company and four different vehicles with the same insurance company. I now highlight all paperwork before I add it to any binder.

In some families, one person takes care of most of the finances. If that person gets sick or injured, the Financial Organizing Binder provides a place to find information about how to keep the household running (bill paying, bank accounts, insurance information, etc.). Ideally, the adults in the home would sit down together a few times a year and review the information in the binder. Note—it is also helpful to have a written list of logins and passwords you update annually that anyone who would need to take over this binder would be able to find.

The biggest challenge I had when settling my father's estate was collecting all his personal information: driver's license number, military ID, mother's maiden name, and contact information for his attorney and accountant. All these details (and others) were asked of me by various financial and legal institutions as I was working through the paperwork after his death. Some of it I had on hand; other pieces of it I needed to track down.

You can save your family a lot of grief if you collect this information in one place. The family information sheet I've developed (page 196) will outline all the necessary basics if someone were acting as power of attorney or executor of an estate. Keep this document safe and secure but accessible. A blank version of this form is available in the Appendix, or you can download it at https://organize365.com/paperbookprintables.

Why *You* Need a Financial Organizing Binder

Financial paperwork can multiply quickly, and if you have not decluttered, you're leaving yourself (or your heirs) a terrible mess to sort through. You will want to check with your own

ADULT – family information sheet

the basics

Name: _____ Date: _____

Maiden Name or Other Names: _____

Address: _____

City: _____ State: _____ Zip: _____

Home Phone: _____ Cell Phone: _____

Birthdate: _____ City / State of Birth: _____

Emergency Contact: _____ Phone: _____

Height: _____ Weight: _____ Social Security #: _____ - _____ - _____

Allergies: _____

Email: _____ 2nd Email: _____

ids

Driver's License #: _____ State: _____

Military/DoD ID: _____

Passport #: _____ Passport location: _____

important people

Spouse's Full Name: _____

Father's Full Name: _____ Birthdate: _____

Mother's Full Name: _____ Birthdate: _____

Employer: _____ Employer Address: _____

_____ Phone: _____

Accountant: _____ Phone: _____

Attorney: _____ Phone: _____

Doctor: _____ Phone: _____

Dentist: _____ Phone: _____

Eye Doctor: _____ Phone: _____

Other Medical Team: _____

Pharmacy: _____ Phone: _____

extras

Preferred Hospital: _____ Phone: _____

High School: _____ Grad Year: _____

College: _____ Grad Year: _____

Other: _____ Completed: _____

health insurance information

primary insurance

☐ Copy of front and back of card

Carrier/Company: _____

Policy #: _____

Group #: _____

Customer Service: _____

Username: _____

Password: _____

supplemental/secondary insurance

☐ Copy of front and back of card

Carrier/Company: _____

Policy #: _____

Group #: _____

Customer Service: _____

Username: _____

Password: _____

medicare primary insurance

☐ Copy of front and back of card

Carrier/Company: _____

Policy #: _____

Group #: _____

Customer Service: _____

Username: _____

Password: _____

medicaid insurance

☐ Copy of front and back of card

Carrier/Company: _____

Policy #: _____

Group #: _____

Customer Service: _____

Username: _____

Password: _____

financial and tax advisers, but many times you do not need to keep every statement for a bank account. I also typically do not keep my statements from my utility bills.

Your Financial Organizing Binder can include copies of things like a car title or the face page of an insurance policy if needed. One of the most important reasons to create your Financial Organizing Binder is to have it in case of an emergency. If you need to stay out of town with an ill or injured relative, imagine how much easier it would be to take this single binder. You can still manage all your finances while being a caregiver. Even more important, many Organize 365 clients have been able to take their completed Financial Organizing Binders with them during an evacuation. The binders have been key to helping people after surviving hurricanes, wildfires, and other natural disasters.

Finally, the Financial Organizing Binder includes instructions and printables to create a household inventory. This is one of those things we all know we *should* do but rarely complete. You have physical possessions that are inside the house and have a value. You may need the records for insurance or replacement or to know how long you have had them. Ideally you will choose the information in your Household Reference Binder to ensure your records are complete and up-to-date.

The Organize 365 Financial Organizing Binder

As you'll see, the family information sheet in chapter 11 makes it easy to record account numbers, vehicle information, and retirement information on one sheet. You will have to spend the

PAPERS TO GATHER

- Bill payment record
- Credit card list
- Debts list
- Estate planning
- Family member financial information
- Financial adviser contact information
- Financial inventory
- Funeral planning
- Gift card information
- Household inventory
- Insurance policy information
- Military records
- Personal identification documents
- Retirement information
- Safe deposit box inventory
- Travel rewards information
- Vehicle information

time and effort to look up and record the information for your financial binder—once. But after you have the information recorded in a single place, you can scan that paper (or even just take a picture of it) and have the information with you in case you need it when you're away from home. You can also set electronic calendar reminders to help you remember when irregular bills are due or to reach out for an updated insurance quote. I recommend updating this Financial Organizing Binder at least once a year. I find that updating finances occurs naturally for me as I am working through my taxes early in the New Year.

Purpose: The Financial Organizing Binder is the place to store all your important financial records and documents in one easy-to-access binder. The Financial Organizing Binder can also be used to store the paperwork for settling an estate.

Create Your Financial Organizing Binder

Here are the slash pockets you will want to include in your Financial Organizing Binder:

- *General Financial Information*
  - *Locations of important paperwork*
  - *Contact information*
  - *Safe-deposit box inventory*

- *Current Money*
  - *Bank information*
  - *Debt worksheet*
  - *Bill payment log*
  - *Vehicle information*

- *Future Money*
  - *Retirement information*

- *Physical Inventory*
  - *Household inventory log*

- *Estate Planning*
  - *Executor checklist*
  - *Financial communication tracker*
  - *Celebration of life planner*

When you are building your binder, focus on the information you need to leave if someone needs to take over the family finances for you. If you are settling an estate for someone else, focus on gathering as much information as possible about assets and debts. Feel free to leave Post-it notes on pages to remind you of the status of an account or the next action you need to take for an item.

Now that your financial picture is taking shape, let's move on to your family's medical records.

CHAPTER 12

Your Medical Organizing Binder

How to Organize Your Medical History and Diagnoses

FACT: 80 percent of our medical expenditures are stress related.

(Centers for Disease Control, as cited in "Surprising Stats," *Simply Orderly*, http://simplyorderly.com/surprising-statistics)

A fellow business owner and I were both at conventions in different states chatting on Voxer, our favorite voice messaging app. It was late, and we were catching up on each other's lives. Betsy was madly printing hundreds of pages of medical information in the hotel business center. Earlier that day, an announcement had been made that CareSync, a voluntary online medical document organization company, was shutting its doors.

The announcement came out of nowhere. Employees were caught completely off guard and not allowed to return to their offices. Betsy was well connected in the computer field and found out immediately, hence the long night of printing. All her medically fragile child's health records were in the Care-Sync database and not backed up anywhere else. She had trusted that company to provide the service she was counting on. For many, this would be a bad night. In my friend's case, it would be a bad three to six months.

You see, her son has been hospitalized over one hundred times, with no end in sight. Having access to the medical records gave her knowledge, control, and what she needed to advocate for her son in the now all-too-common crisis situations. He has medical conditions that require frequent hospitalizations and changes in treatment.

While many of us have good intentions to get our paperwork organized on our never-ending to-do lists, Betsy had actually finished her project. She gathered, organized, and digitized all her son's medical records. When I checked in with her, she was racing the clock to print hundreds of pages of information. This was information she did not want to have to find again, nor was she sure she could.

I'm not sure what happened with other CareSync customers, but Betsy was able to get all her records downloaded that weekend. She now has all her son's medical records in an Organize 365 Medical Organizing Binder as a backup for the next digital solution she finds. I want to be sure you also have what you need to take care of the health concerns for yourself and for anyone you may have to be a caregiver for.

Depending on your generation and comfort with technology, you may have different expectations of the way you track medical information. More and more hospitals and doctors' offices are offering online access to test results, prescription re-fills, and communication with our healthcare providers. How-ever, there is still some amount of paperwork that must be kept. And this can be an even bigger challenge when a Millennial is caring for a Baby Boomer or even a member of the Silent Gen-eration. Although those over sixty-five years old are only about 12 percent of the US population, they are responsible for 35 percent of hospitalizations and even more (38 percent) of emer-gency room visits.[1]

A Medical Organizing Binder takes all the paperwork that previously covered our kitchen counters and filled our filing cabinets and streamlines it into one simple binder that keeps it easy to reference. Even for people who are comfortable and skilled in using digital resources, having a portable, personal medical record can be a lifesaver. Literally.

Using Your Medical Organizing Binder

Each binder is set up in the same order, making it easy to up-date with relevant information and also to see what papers or documentation you are missing. Many of us can actually end up becoming caregivers for several people in our lives, some-times even at the same time. Keeping the paperwork organized can feel like a full-time job, but having a separate binder for each person will keep us organized. Many of us at one point in our lives will need to advocate for ourselves or a loved one. While the medical care is often out of our control, we can gain confidence in taking good notes, keeping track of test results, and asking clarifying questions.

As my father was passing away, my sister and I sought solace in understanding and tracking several of his medical condition markers. Having a place to track that data was super important so we could track if his health was improving or declining. After he was moved into hospice, we regularly met in the hallway to review the list we were given that helped us understand the symptoms and changes that occur in the body as death approaches. Knowledge is power. We were powerless over his passing, but we were given a feeling of control through the knowledge of what was happening.

In addition to being a caregiver for my own father, I have raised two children who both had some heavy medical needs. I created a separate Medical Organizing Binder for each of my children. From the time they arrived, my children had frequent medical appointments and a large team helping them to thrive in life. I built a habit where I would take along a binder for each child *every* time I went to a doctor or a school appointment. I would add and delete with each new stage of life. But I always had the reference information at my fingertips for my kids. This meant that I could often "prove" or provide documentation that probably should have been in their records. However, the most important thing for me was getting my kids the care and services they needed, not fighting the systems.

My client Amy has been a nurse practitioner for fourteen years. She works in family practice, and most of her job involves managing patient care. She shared with me that when patients bring their records from their outside providers—pulmonologist, cardiologist, neurologist, etc.—it's like the heavens part and an angel comes down! OK, maybe not literally, but Amy feels that way because she can then better coordinate her patient's care and make sure to not duplicate prescriptions, tests, or other procedures. This saves everyone time and money—and, most important, results in better care for the patient.

Eliminate more of your paperwork by taking the important information and transferring it to a centralized document. This one-page medical information sheet is a great place to start in your Medical Organizing Binder. Fill one out for each of your family members, and use it when you meet a new doctor for the first time or send your adult child off to college or to live on their own.

You can print a medical information sheet at https://organize365.com/paperbookprintables.

Why *You* Need a Medical Organizing Binder

Whenever you take on caregiving responsibilities for another human, you need to have an organized way to store, access, and maintain the multitude of information that will come your way. Although I often recommend discarding 80 to 90 percent of paperwork, I save almost everything (at least for a while) when it comes to medical paperwork. Although it seems that our healthcare providers should have accurate records,

ADULT – one-page MEDICAL information sheet

Name: _____

Birthdate: _____ Age: _____ Height: _____ Weight: _____

Address: _____

Emergency Contact: _____ Phone: _____

Backup Emergency Contact: _____ Phone: _____

Caregiver Name: _____ Phone: _____

Primary Doctor Name: _____ Phone: _____

Insurance Information: _____

Preferred Hospital: _____

Dentist: _____ Phone: _____

Dental Insurance Information: _____

....

other important healthcare providers

Name: _____ Phone: _____

Name: _____ Phone: _____

Name: _____ Phone: _____

....

medical problems	medications/treatments
☐ _____	☐ _____
☐ _____	☐ _____
☐ _____	☐ _____

| allergies/to avoid | medical equipment
(oxygen, wheelchair, etc.) |
|---|---|
| ☐ _____ | ☐ _____ |
| ☐ _____ | ☐ _____ |
| ☐ _____ | ☐ _____ |

immunization record	other important health information
☐ _____	☐ _____
☐ _____	☐ _____
☐ _____	☐ _____

sadly that's often not the case. Many times, 'the electronic medical records do not connect from one provider to another. Physicians' offices and hospitals use a variety of different record-keeping programs, and they are often unable to integrate. Furthermore, medical errors can be deadly. The third leading cause of death in the US is attributed to medical errors.[2] This was *with* an electronic medical record in place to help catch errors.

As you are eliminating your filing cabinets and getting rid of the piles of paper taking over the flat surfaces in your house, the *best* way to organize medical paperwork is into a separate, discreet, dedicated binder for each individual. Gathering and organizing the medical and caregiving information into a Medical Organizing Binder puts all the records you need into a single book where you can keep everything at your fingertips and also transport it as needed when going to appointments. I created my binders almost eighteen years ago and have been updating and refining them regularly.

Depending on how fast the medical condition of your caregiving recipient is changing, your Medical Organizing Binder may change rapidly. You may receive a new diagnosis. You may be recording the intended symptoms and side effects of quickly adjusted medication regimens. Your loved one may be trying new diets, and you may need to record either behaviors or symptoms. You may even need to transport medical records from one member of the care team to another.

My client Reneé started a Medical Organizing Binder when her husband was diagnosed with an aggressive cancer. She completed his medical history and added all documentation she could find for his family and personal history, including his current prescription list. The Medical Organizing Binder did not change the cancer diagnosis, but Reneé felt more in control and prepared to help her husband in his fight.

Along the way, the medical teams she encountered asked where she learned to make her binder. They wanted to suggest it to other patients. Like Amy, the medical team was grateful to have easy access to his records to avoid misinformation, to track his care, and to remember conversations after the fact. For instance, there were times when a protocol or treatment was discussed but not used. Reneé found it helpful to have detailed notes of those conversations—especially later, as the cancer progressed and questions were raised as to what treatments had been tried when, and why another path had been chosen.

Thankfully, Reneé's husband's prognosis is very good. She is now using the Medical Organizing Binder to track all his medical bills and insurance payments.

The Organize 365 Medical Organizing Binder

The Medical Organizing Binder is one of the most customizable and detailed binders to set up. I recommend you create one for each member of your family, including yourself. The contents of your slash pockets will vary depending on the medical diagnoses and issues you are managing. I want you to customize each binder for *your* life, home, and family. If you and your family are healthy, you may find that there is very little medical information in your Medical Organizing Binders.

PAPERS TO GATHER

- Allergy list
- Caregiver information
- Doctor contact information
- Family medical history
- Hospitalization history
- Immunization history
- Lab results
- Medical diagnoses list
- Medication list
- Personal medical and health history
- Surgical history

That's great (and you're fortunate!). Use the remaining space to include what you need in order to be the caregiver for your family. I would recommend that you include summer camp information, sports or activities information, or anything else relating to your or your family's health into the binder.

To create your Medical Organizing Binder, you will need to cast a wide net and go through old files and paper storage to gather up medical information. The goal is to condense as much as possible onto recording sheets and to keep copies of important documents in an easy-to-use storage solution. You can set electronic calendar reminders to check back for an updated report, to keep track of prescription refills, or to schedule a follow-up appointment.

Purpose: The Medical Organizing Binder is the place to store all the important documents you need to be the best possible caregiver for another person, in one easy-to-access binder. The binder should be used to keep all your medical paperwork organized. I sometimes refer to this as a caregiving binder. The Medical Organizing Binder is most helpful when someone else needs to step in and support the medical care decisions on your behalf. Additionally, if you have been thrust into the caregiving role, assembling a binder will help you ask better questions and keep track of important information for all decisions made in the care of your loved one.

Create Your Medical Organizing Binder

Here are the slash pockets you will want to consider when building your Medical Organizing Binder:

- *Health History*
  - *Personal medical history*
  - *Family medical history*
  - *Immunization records*
  - *Lab results*

- *Current Health*
  - *Contact information for medical team*
  - *Allergy tracker*
  - *Diagnoses tracker*

- *Medications*
  - *Current medication list*
  - *Past medications tried and failed*

- *Health Trackers*

As you are building your binder, focus on the information someone would need to take over the care of your child or loved one or you. Try to get everything out of your head, and write down as many facts, memories, and experiences as you can remember.

CHAPTER 13

Your Household Operations Binder

How to Organize Your Family's Fun and Daily Living

FACT: Getting rid of excess clutter would eliminate 40 percent of the housework in an average home.

(Soap and Detergent Association, as cited in Joshua Becker, "The Statistics of Clutter," *Becoming Minimalist,* https://www.becomingminimalist.com/the-statistics-of-clutter)

Chaos.

Two children under two. Need I say more?

"My kids' toddler years were the hardest part of my parenting journey," confided my client Liza. "The constant demands on my time to actually keep these two alive were exhausting. Nothing was getting checked off my to-do list, and I was certain I would forget a major holiday or event because I forgot to plan it or put it on my calendar. The Sunday Basket got me started, but I needed a playbook to follow. Like the teacher lesson plans I made at school, I needed a lesson plan for our family."

The Household Operations Binder was Liza's solution. Inside she kept all the school papers and recurring events her family participated in year after year. Once she made this binder, she finally turned the corner from reacting to everyone else's demands on her time to proactively anticipating and preparing for the memorable events her family would remember for decades to come. "The Household Operations Binder doesn't just make my day-to-day run smoother," she said, "it also helps me remember and create lifetime memories."

There are two household binders. The Household Reference Binder we talked about in chapter 10 is about taking care of your house like it is a person. The Household Operations Binder is the lesson plan or the teacher's guide for your household. It does not have anything to do with the structure or contents of the home. It is about the orchestration of events for the people who live inside it over time. You will plan different things for summer break than you will for the winter holidays.

Many adults in the US are currently experiencing the "sandwich" generation phenomenon. They have aging parents (and other relatives), and they have children at home. Currently only 40 percent of Millennials have children under eighteen at home, but they are still working and often live in multigenerational homes.[1]

Using Your Household Operations Binder

Each binder is set up in the same order but is fully customizable depending on your home, family, and lifestyle. The Household Operations Binder helps keep the running of your home

PAPERS TO GATHER

- Basic household information
- Car supply checklist
- Childcare contact information
- Contractor contact information
- Emergency information
- Evacuation planning
- Family clothing sizes
- Frequently used service providers
- Holiday planners
- Home maintenance checklists
- Home maintenance log
- Housecleaning checklists
- Houseguest checklists
- Important dates
- Master grocery list
- Meal-planning information
- Party planners
- Pet information
- Road trip planners
- Summer planners
- Teen driver logs
- Utility company information

organized no matter where or how you live. It will work for a person living in a shared housing situation with roommates or a parent living with small kids. It's suitable for a house where all the adults work and one where at least one person is home, or even when someone works from home.

The Household Operations Binder equips you to be the CEO—Chief Entertainment Officer or Celebrating Experiences Orchestrator—of your home. It is a handbook and operations guide for running your home and family. It is especially helpful when you have young children or frequent non-family members in your home. It would be helpful if you have house sitters, frequent guests, or pet sitters who stay in your home (like an Airbnb). The binder contains all the things that help keep the family unit running smoothly, and it provides FAQ-type information to anyone who might step in and help out with the family.

The Household Operations Binder gives one place to store your frequently referenced information for keeping your house and family functioning. The binder is the place to keep information like your trash pickup schedule, an information sheet for a babysitter, emergency information (water main location, gas shutoff, etc.), and meal planning.

As a former teacher who decorated her classroom for every season, I love to do the same for my home. When my kids were younger, I also had filing cabinets with seasonal crafts to try and new things to do for each holiday. When I actually went through my files, I found that I had only eight to ten actual pieces of paper in each folder. It was much easier to move the things I still wanted to keep into sheet protectors and place them in the binder. I divided them by season and could easily reference them without digging through (or, really, forgetting them completely inside) my filing cabinet.

This binder was primarily created by my team who have active families and events they are organizing. I have a confession. Of all the binders I make and teach about in this book, the Household Operations Binder is the most challenging for me. It is most likely because I do not see myself as a "fun" mom. But that does not mean I do not want to get better at the fun stuff, and this binder is really helping me do that. My goal with this binder is to gain more control of our family fun, including things like holidays and travel. And as I always tell you to do, I customized this binder. I created a special slash pocket for our dog, Hunter, so I could keep his paperwork in one place. Now I definitely lean to the side of decluttering, so I keep little paperwork for our dog. I honestly rely on our vet to keep track of most of his paperwork. However, I do need at least the rabies information, and I recorded the kind of food we use in case someone else needs to access the information if I am incapacitated.

Have you ever forgotten a birthday or special event? That is my worst fear!

The important-dates tracker on pages 218–219 will help you see when all your family's important celebration moments are throughout the year so you don't miss a single one!

You can print a copy at https://organize365.com /paperbookprintables.

Why *You* Need a Household Operations Binder

As you are eliminating your filing cabinets, the Household Operations Binder allows you to put much of your frequently referenced paperwork into one place. Even if you have most of this household stuff "dialed down," it's useful to have it documented in one place in case anyone needs to step into your role for any reason in the future.

My client Mary is a single mom to an eleven-year-old daughter. A few years ago, Mary had to move out-of-state, away from any family and friends, for work. She explained to me: "When you are a single parent with a demanding career that requires frequent travel, you have to have a system for everything. When I am traveling, the nanny has to have the resources to manage everything while I am gone. No longer can everything be in my head. It needed to be on paper that was easily accessible. I started with a Medical Organizing Binder for my daughter, then went to the Financial Organizing Binder, Household Reference Binder, and Household Operations Binder. My nanny now has all the information she needs when she is managing the household."

Although our culture is changing, the reality is that often the burden of keeping the home and family organized falls on women. But no matter who is taking the lead in orchestrating home life, every family needs to have a place for all the adults to reliably find the information they need to keep the family running smoothly. And once a system like this is established, it's easier to share and fairly distribute the work of maintaining a household.

important-dates tracker

January	February	March

April	May	June

important-dates tracker

	July		August		September

	October		November		December

I have many clients who travel frequently, who have complicated schedules, or who just want a reliable way to remember the important dates and details that dictate family life. A Household Operations Binder is a repository for all that important information.

The Organize 365 Household Operations Binder

This is where you will keep detailed checklists and information to help you have an organized home. For example, there is a place to list your family's favorite meals grouped by main ingredient and then by theme. That way, you can meal-plan using either to ensure a variety of healthy meals. The binder also includes a place to record your favorite sources for takeout meals, and you can include copies of the menu inside the slash pockets that come with the binder.

Purpose: The Household Operations Binder is the place to store all the information that you need to keep your household operating in an organized fashion in one easy-to-access binder.

Create Your Household Operations Binder

Here are the slash pockets you will want to include in your Household Operations Binder:

- *General Household Information*
  - *Family information*
  - *Pet information*

- *Emergency information*
- *Important-dates tracker*

- *Meal Planning*
  - *Meal-planning tips*
  - *Weekly meal planner*
  - *Master grocery list*

- *Housecleaning*
  - *Checklists for weekly and seasonal cleaning*

- *Household Maintenance*
  - *Contact information for service providers*
  - *Home improvement wishlist*
  - *Instructions for infrequently performed tasks*

- *Holiday and Event Planning*
  - *Summer*
  - *Holidays*
  - *Parties*

When you are building your binder, you can include any information you might need—or your family might need, if you were not there to answer all their questions—to have at your fingertips for easy reference. These are papers you do not need to take action on but you do want to have handy.

CHAPTER 14

Your School Memory Binder

How to Organize Childhood and School Memories

....

Out of clutter, find simplicity.

—Albert Einstein

....

As a mom of two and former preschool teacher, I know how precious those handprint turkeys and first scribbled drawings are. And while you can readily give up past copies of utility bills, school papers are much harder.

Remember my client back in chapter 3 with over one hundred memory bins of school papers? Her six children ranged in age from nine to twenty-four. She had saved every spelling test, math paper, newsletter, and more, chronicled by grade and child. Every paper had meaning. But she could not distinguish between necessary and unnecessary papers to keep. I asked her to trust me to make the decisions and turn her organized storage boxes into School Memory Binders her kids would look at.

She agreed, and I took multiple carloads of bins back to my house. A few months later, I had created one to three binders for each child. I had seen this so many times before that I knew what would happen, and yet I was giddy with anticipation of the call I knew was coming.

I brought the new binders over to the house and left them in the family room while everyone was at school and work. That night the call came. In tears, my client said, "The kids have been looking at those binders for hours. They are telling stories I never knew about from school. Now they are looking at each other's binders. I can't believe how powerful these are!"

A simple change from a box to a binder made those memories, stories, and shared experiences come alive. Our papers have more meaning than we realize.

So, how do you decide what to keep and what to discard?

One of the questions I get all the time as a professional organizer and as a teacher is, "What do I do with all those papers and projects my kids bring home?" The reality is, our kids can bury us in papers all by themselves. Young kids under five years old are often creating at home or day care. We get so many precious projects that their little hands have made. Sometimes they draw pictures of our family. Sometimes they make adorable little turkey handprints. Sometimes they make a giant village of old boxes. Sometimes they get the cutest little certificates from school. As the kids get older, they write stories, they create new worlds, and they grow. Everything holds a memory for either the child or the parent. Some families keep math worksheets and spelling tests, too.

Depending on how hard-won the school skills are, these can be treasures, too!

Many parents never decide. We tend to err on pitching it all or keeping every last piece. The irony is that no one is wading through tubs and boxes of school memorabilia and reliving their youth. So often our kids do not even have memories of their fantastic creations. By the time we do get to sorting through our kids' works of art, they are often parents themselves and no longer care about, or have space for, their turkey handprint.

A binder (or two) per child can be the solution to the boxes, files, and piles of paper that children generate. A binder can help keep the papers organized, put away, and act as a limit to how much can be stored in one home.

Using Your School Memory Binder

By using a binder, you and your child can look through old creations and see how much they have grown. The page protectors in the binder keep the masterpieces safe and secure. When kids are able to see that their best work is valued, they continue to work hard and also learn to make decisions about what things to save.

A binder for art and memories helps us to focus on and identify what is the best and most precious to keep. As parents, we learn from this decision-making process, *and* we have a chance to practice these skills with our children. The reality of life is that we cannot keep everything, and not every item is of the same value as the rest. In using this binder, we learn to give ourselves permission to make decisions about what to keep and learn to let go of the rest. Furthermore, the binder can be arranged by school year or age, and this helps us to keep our important memories organized.

Why *You* Need a School Memory Binder

Here is my best hint for you: the magic is in making your child's School Memory Binder while they are still in school. The sweet spot is late grade school, but anytime during childhood will mean that both you *and* your kids enjoy the binder and the memories.

When I used to make School Memory Binders for my professional organization clients, I found the same thing happened over and over. Within a week, the client would call and recount the number of times they and their children would sit down together and look through the binders. Often the kids would just flip pages, but they would also stop to tell stories. The kids began to feel their work was more meaningful when Mom and Dad were proud enough to save it in the special binder. Other times, kids would remember a friend who helped with a project. And as parents, we were finally able to see how far their skills progressed as we saw their work collected from preschool through middle school.

Sometimes it can be helpful to keep a worksheet or a coloring page as a marker of progress. But I always recommend saving anything with a child's handprint or story about the family. That work is always priceless. Now it is also shared and treasured anytime they want.

Purpose: The School Memory Binder is the place to store

school memory binder

Calendar Year	Age	Grade in School	School Year	Notes

all precious art, school, and memory pages for your child in an organized fashion in one easy-to-access binder.

The most complicated part of creating a School Memory Binder when your children are older is organizing their work in chronological order. Now, this step is not necessary—you can create a binder of their favorites in no particular order—but if you want to organize them, the printable on page 226 is a game changer.

To help you organize your saved school papers, this downloadable school tracker will help you more easily sort them by grade and age. You can download the printable at https://organize365.com/paperbookprintables.

Create Your School Memory Binder

The School Memory Binder is one of the easiest binders to make, though the decluttering and deciding can be very difficult. For children, so much of their growth and identity is based on what school grade they are in. Divide the binder into sections based on their school grade. You can include a three-year-old's or four-year-old's preschool if desired. Then begin with kindergarten, first grade, and so on. Put the most important pages into the page protectors for each year.

As previously mentioned, the easiest way to do this binder is to begin and use it as your children are in school. Depending on the volume of papers that come into the house, you will want an initial storage inbox for the papers as they arrive. A Sunday Basket is a great spot for this, especially if your kids want to "be like Mom." As time passes before you declutter the pages, kids are often less attached and it is easier to let go of old papers. Some families will sort papers monthly, or you can save them all for the summer. As best you can, try to keep most of the worksheets and disposable busy work out of the collection box. The focus is on saving important work and memories. The older the child, the more involved he or she should be in the decisions about what to keep. Even young children can sort papers into different categories, including math, stories, pictures, holidays, and so on. Once you have your categories established, work to decide which are the best one to three items of each type, and insert them into the binder. You can add an index card or a Post-it note to include a memory or to provide some context for the item.

Depending on how much paper storage space you have in your home, you may want to set limits. If you tell a child that he or she can save ten to twenty pages from a particular school year, then the child can help decide which things are most important or the best work. However, do not be alarmed that you have many papers in the early years. As children mature and schoolwork becomes more focused on curriculum content, there will be much less creative memory-type pages. As a mom, I always elected to save creative stories and things with handprints or footprints no matter what. And I wanted to save things that were their "firsts" of different things—like the first time a kid wrote his or her name.

As you work through your own paperwork in the house, you can also elect to create a similar memory binder for yourself and your spouse. This can be an especially good way to organize papers if you have received a bunch of your own childhood paperwork from your own parents. When things are in binders, they are so much easier to enjoy and flip through. You might be amazed at how interested your children are in your own drawings, stories, or memories. Or, they might not be. Kids are unpredictable!

CHAPTER 15

Your IEP Binder

How to Organize Your Child's School and Medical Records

Many years ago, I had a friend who was frustrated while trying to get her child the educational services she *knew* the child needed. I already had some experience advocating for kids during an IEP meeting, so I went with her. She and I had discussed her child's educational and medical history at length, and I knew her child should be receiving more services. While I am not a medical doctor, I *am* a teacher and experienced advocate who knows what services are available for specific medical diagnoses and how to read educational tests and IQ reports like a pro. I'd been helping my friend collect the necessary materials I knew she'd need to make her case.

When we walked into the meeting, the staff would not make eye contact with me. They focused on the child's mom, as they should have. The meeting started out with the typical "We can't xyz because there is no funding," or "Your child doesn't need it." This went on for only a few minutes, and the mom looked at me as if to say, "See? They won't give me what you said my child should have." I asked her if I could speak on her behalf, to which she said of course.

I then made the same exact three requests: extended school year (summer school), an aide in all classes, and a computer. The administration started their "We can't . . ." line of reply with me, and I pulled out the child's IQ test, which referenced short- and long-term working memory scores showing a deficiency to substantiate summer school. OK, they said they could do that, and with paid bussing, since Mom worked full time and was a single parent. First one down.

Next, I went after the computer. It was a low cost with a high return for the child. When your working memory score on your IQ test is low, typing can speed up retention and the ability to get your thoughts on paper. My argument was that at this point, the goal of education was to find out what the child was retaining, not their penmanship. Granted.

But no way were they going to give her an aide. Until thirty minutes later, when they did. I'd pulled out one piece of documentation after another from my friend's IEP Binder, refuting each claim the administration made. In the end, they had no choice but to comply with the law—and give my friend's child the resources they were entitled to.

I don't blame the administrators—not really. Like it or not, the funds in public school are tight. But what I've learned is that if your child needs extra resources, you are going to have to learn what they need, why they need them, and then make your case. Being nice won't cut it. You also have to be an advocate. And proper documentation in the form of an IEP Binder is essential.

One of my very first organization tasks was to create a binder to help keep paperwork organized for my own children. Not only did my kids have medical needs in early childhood, but both of them ended up needing special help in the school environment. In my early years of building my business, I had a blog called Warrior MAMA. MAMA was an acronym for Managing All Medical Alternatives. With my children, we tried all kinds of supplements, elimination diets, and other treatments. Some were successful; some were not. I ended up becoming a non-degreed expert in many of the treatments available for their medical conditions.

The Organize 365 IEP Binder is called the Warrior MAMA Binder. There have been some concerns about my choice of the word "warrior" for this binder. I want to just take a few words to explain why "warrior" resonates with me. My children both have unique and special learning needs, and figuring out what is best for them has taken all of us down a difficult but worthwhile path. I had to learn to be a warrior when I was advocating for my children. Most professionals are doing their best, but no one knows our children and understands their needs like their parents. I am not encouraging you to see the school or the teacher as the enemy, but I am giving you permission to be determined and stubborn in advocating for your children. Your children need you to help them get what will be the best for them.

Why an IEP Binder?

The IEP Binder keeps the paperwork of educational needs together in one place. It is suitable for any kind of developmental delay, emotional challenge, or cognitive impairment. If your child's challenge is solely a physical disability, and there are no learning challenges, then you most likely can use the Medical Organizing Binder. However, as soon as you need to advocate for accommodations in the school district, the IEP Binder is the right choice.

If your child has an invisible disability like autism or ADHD, it can be incredibly hard on your own emotional and mental health as a parent. Depending on the need for structure and the behaviors of your child, you may find that you struggle with isolation, depression, or other challenges as a parent. There is not a lot of compassion toward "invisible" disabilities that look like behavior problems. I want to change that, and I think it starts with this binder.

Having all your educational and medical paperwork together in one supporting binder helps you to speak up when asking for what your child needs. Unfortunately, in our current world, the documentation provided by a professional (physician, therapist, or similar person) holds much more weight in "proving" your child needs services than your own observations and experiences as a parent. Having letters from these professionals, copies of their reports, documentation of test results, and similar paperwork in an organized location will help you to support your requests for assistance from the school. And when you have a binder full of documentation and support, the school never knows what you will be able to pull out of the binder. Although it is not a fight, it does increase your power and authority and confidence in the conversation.

Why *You* Need an IEP Binder

In the United States, the Individuals with Disabilities Education Act (IDEA) was enacted in 1975 and requires that all eligible students from ages three to twenty-one are provided a free appropriate public education (FAPE).[1] However, different states and different school districts have interpreted and enacted these laws in different ways. According to the National Center for Education Statistics, about 13 percent of students receive special education services.[2] These include learning disabilities, speech or language impairments, health impairments, autism, emotional disturbances, and more.[3] The current government data reports that one in five US households has at least one child with special needs.[4]

When you request an evaluation for your child by the school, your child's strengths and learning needs are assessed and diagnosed. Then appropriate accommodations and modifications are put in place and recorded on a legally binding document. Depending on the type of disability or need, your child may receive an education plan that is called a 504 Plan (named after section 504 of the Rehabilitation Act of 1973) or an Individualized Education Program (IEP). Again, different states and school districts have different rules and procedures for developing these plans. It is not in the scope of this book to discuss the details of these plans. For more information, please check out https://www2.ed.gov/about/offices/list/ocr/docs/edlite -FAPE504.html.

With all the testing, diagnoses, and accommodation plans comes a *lot* of paperwork. Depending on your child's health and learning needs, you may have a 504 or an IEP for a short while. Other children will have them all the way until graduation or adulthood. Based on my own experience teaching in a classroom and advocating for my own children, I think the best way to organize and store this paperwork is in a binder.

Why a binder? When you walk into an IEP meeting with a binder, you instantly command respect from the other members in that meeting. The administrator, educator, interventionist, psychologist, and whoever else might be in that room with you will respond to that collection of papers. You know your stuff, and you are not there to play. I have even counseled parents to bring a *random* binder into those meetings, and they all report even a binder without paper pertaining to the meeting has improved their ability to obtain what their children need for optimal learning.

This binder is designed to support parents of children under the age of approximately twenty-five so you can advocate for their needs during their growing-up years. If you remain the guardian of an adult child, you may find some parts helpful, but the binder is not optimally designed for that situation.

Using Your IEP Binder

I have been (and continue to be) a Warrior MAMA for my children. I am committed to helping them become independent adults and to learn to the best of *their* abilities. Many members of my team also have kids in their lives who have special needs (children, nieces, nephews, and other important family connections). This binder was made as a team effort when many people pooled together their own experiences, resources, frustrations, and learning to make a binder that would help a parent with a new diagnosis navigate the maze of special education.

ABC pediatric therapy network

ABC Pediatric Therapy Network
"creating the best life for all children"

Gross Motor Skills	Fine Motor Skills	Speech
By 4 Months	**By 4 Months**	**By 4 Months**
___ Bears weight on forearms when on belly	___ Grasps rattle when placed in hand	___ Sucks from breast or bottle
___ Plays with feet	___ Reaches toward and touches toy	___ Cooing: vowel sounds
___ Holds head in midline	___ Hits at dangling objects with hands	___ Vocalizes some sounds
___ Rolls from back to side	___ Responds to a smile with a smile	___ Produces a variety of facial expressions
___ Brings hands together when lying on back	___ Likes looking at a human face most	
By 6 Months	**By 6 Months**	**By 6 Months**
___ Sits alone for short periods	___ Reaches for a toy when playing on belly	___ Cup drinking is introduced
___ Begins to belly crawl	___ Holds a toy and shakes it	___ Soft, smooth solids
___ Rolls back to belly and belly to back	___ Puts fingers in mouth	___ Moves chewed food to center of mouth before swallowing
___ Grabs feet and brings them to mouth	___ Holds hands open at least half of the time	
___ On belly props up on straight elbows	___ Smiles at self in mirror	
By 9 Months	**By 9 Months**	**By 9 Months**
___ Maintains sitting for at least 60 seconds with hands free to play	___ Waves bye-bye	___ Babbles same sounds
___ Crawls independently	___ Releases objects intentionally	___ Responds to "no"
___ Pulls to stand from floor	___ Feeds self finger foods	___ Vocalizes different syllables
___ Walks with hands held	___ Bangs a toy on the floor	___ Tolerates smooth solid foods
	___ Passes a small object between hands	___ Makes sounds while eating with food in mouth
By 12 Months	**By 12 Months**	**By 12 Months**
___ Cruises along furniture	___ Grasps thick crayon or pencil in fist, does not mark	___ Feeding self with fingers
___ Independent standing	___ Turns pages of a cardboard book	___ Babbles using different sounds
___ Gets into and out of sitting	___ Helps to pull off simple clothing	___ Takes turns vocalizing
___ Corrals a ball with arms and hands in sitting	___ Puts objects into others	___ Points/gestures
___ Transitions sit to stand and stand to sit	___ Pulls shoes off	___ Tolerates coarsely chopped food

My formal college degree is in the field of early childhood education and elementary education. The early-childhood portion of this dual major exposed me to many studies and understandings of how a child develops and how we can observe the development of the child's brain through how they play, move, and draw. With this knowledge, I used developmental trackers, like the one on page 236 from ABC Pediatric Therapy Network, to help me give voice to real developmental concerns and ease my anxiety when my expectations were beyond what I should expect for a child developmentally. I would regularly check these benchmarks to make sure I was advocating appropriately and with the correct level of concern.

You can find a developmental checklist to track your child's skills at https://organize365.com/paperbookprintables.

I wanted to ensure that parents could have a binder that contains their child's pertinent medical, psychological, and education information. The better you can advocate for what your child needs and how he or she learns, the more productive the 504 or IEP meeting will be. The IEP Binder is designed to give you confidence in advocating for your child and in organizing the paperwork that documents your experience with your child. Parents know what is right for their child, but this binder ensures that you have the paperwork and documentation to prove it.

Creating Your IEP Binder

I actually include fifteen slash pockets in my kids' IEP binders. I have a set of five I use for medical paperwork and diagnoses, a set of five for educational tests and evaluations, and another set of five for our current year's plan, samples, notes, and goals. An additional five slash pockets are in my Sunday Basket to track medical and educational expenses and specialists' appointments and services. If you feel as though meeting your child's IEP needs is a full-time job, you are correct. It is a full-time job and one you will never regret accepting with vigor. Give this binder the attention and resources it needs to help you advocate for your child's best possible future.

The IEP Binder is the way to keep your child's disability and IEP/504 paperwork organized. It includes categories for:

- *Diagnoses*
- *Educational accommodations, goals, and evaluations*
- *Your child's support team*
- *Finances*

I take time each summer to update my kids' IEP Binders (at the same time I update the Medical Organizing Binders) before a new school year. I keep their school records, medical records, and all testing in one binder. That binder goes with me to all doctors' and school appointments. Each field impacts the other, and the more you can network those resources together, the better you can care for your child's medical and educational needs.

Trust your gut. If you "know" something is wrong, seek out answers. No one knows your child the way you do!

Part IV

how to
archive the rest

CHAPTER 16

The (Right) Way to Archive Papers

Where to Store the Stuff You Just Can't Part With

FACT: A total of 3,680 hours or 153 days is spent searching for stuff, over our lifetimes.

("Lost Something Already Today? Misplaced Items Cost Us Ten Minutes a Day," *Daily Mail*, https://www.dailymail.co.uk/news/article-2117987 /Lost-today-Misplaced-items-cost-minutes-day.html)

When Kim started her paper-organizing journey, she had boxes and boxes of paper, receipts and records all boxed up in the basement plus paper in over one hundred files in file drawers and piles. Her biggest problem was having no system to think through or end goal to work toward that wasn't a filing system.

Today she uses the Sunday Basket system, with four binders and some paper files scanned to digital files. Almost all her old boxes of paper have been eliminated from her home. Through her paper-organizing process she came to understand her paper: she confidently knows what each paper is, why she does or doesn't need to keep it, which binder the information should be stored in, and how to eliminate what doesn't belong.

Unexpectedly, Kim's household productivity increased after tackling her paper mountain, and to her surprise, she is now able to work through the Paper Solution process with others. The decision-making issues that flummoxed her before are no longer daunting.

She lamented that she wished she had solved her paper-organization problem during the most hectic and overwhelming time in her life, when she had a full-time job, two small kids, and a husband who was home only part time. But thirty years later, she is glad it is finally *done*!

Once you have your active papers in your Sunday Basket and your reference papers filed away in your binders, what is left? Honestly, for most of my clients, there is not much. The only things now in the filing cabinet are taxes and some legal-size paperwork that comes from things like real estate sales or divorce filings. Maybe you need to hang on to this sort of paperwork for legal or business reasons. For these sorts of very specific papers, you have my permission to (very rarely) archive them. But how?

I've made my feelings about filing cabinets known: get 'em out of your house! Rather than using filing cabinets, I recommend just using bankers' boxes or portable plastic file boxes and putting them away in a storage room. Paper is as safe in a file box as it would be inside a filing cabinet. Taxes tend to be too bulky to easily store in a binder, but if you have simple tax paperwork, I would strongly consider migrating that to a binder as well.

If you really need something safe from water and fire, you

need to secure it appropriately. Most of the things you would save in your personal archives will not be needed again. If you *do* need an item someday, it is just as easy to grab the file box from the storage room. As always, I recommend using your best judgment when you consider your home, your family, and your paper. If you choose to use cardboard boxes, please know that those tend to attract more insects and vermin, so there is some risk that your stored paper may be damaged over the years.

Tax Return Organizing Tips

Each person's tax documentation needs are unique. At a minimum, you need to keep the paper copies of your tax returns for at least seven years. You also want to compare your tax returns to your Social Security statements.

I keep our taxes in the bottom of a lateral file. I know, that is not what I just recommended for you, but our filing cabinet is out of the way, we have the space for it, and taxes are the only thing I keep in there. Honestly, I go in the filing cabinet only once a year in order to file our taxes, and I do not have anything else cluttering it up. We have lots of tax documentation for the items we write off for my home-based business, medical deductions, donations, childcare payments, and physical donation photos and receipts. I keep *everything* for seven years. I put each year's paper into a manila envelope with the prepared tax return. I label the front of the envelope with the year of the return and file them with the most recent in the front. Now, I know I *can* shred it all at the seven-year mark, but I love that I can look at our tax returns all the way back to our first jobs! There is some great historical data there. And when it comes to the IRS, when in doubt, I recommend *keeping* it.

I am not a tax professional. I frequently reference the IRS website at https://www.irs.gov/businesses/small-businesses-self-employed/how-long-should-i-keep-records for current tax laws about document retention.

After seven years, my tax returns become sentimental memorabilia for me. I move all the older tax returns into a bankers' box for my "someday" enjoyment and get it out of my current tax-organization drawer. When I enjoy my walk down memory lane, I do occasionally find old records I can shred. My organization is never totally finished forever.

Calendars can also be useful tax documentation if you are ever audited. You can print the prior year's calendar when you file your taxes and add it to the envelope. That way, if your electronic calendar source ever fails, you will have a copy. Again, I do *not* mess with the IRS.

Safe-Worthy Documents

For many years, I kept all our priceless paper (like birth certificates) in a file drawer along with all the other files. I knew I should buy a safe, but I waited a very long time. Full disclosure: my interest in buying a safe was more to keep papers safe in the event of a fire; it was not about preventing theft. I honestly do not worry much about my paper being stolen.

As you know from the rest of this book, I am a very functional organizer. I prefer to have my papers easily accessible rather than worrying about keeping them locked up. I do not recommend that you write all your log-in and password information in your binders. I am not paranoid about writing my driver's license number or the name of my bank in my binder. But I am a work-from-home mom, and I no longer have babysitters or strangers in my home. My dog goes to day care, so there is not a dog walker inside my home unsupervised. I feel comfortable keeping our passports inside the house. I also understand that almost everything *can* be replaced with some combination of time and money if absolutely necessary.

Only you can decide how you want to store your most vital paperwork. Please use your best judgment and protect your safety, privacy, and security. Depending on what works best for you, you may want to consider a small portable safe, a larger safe bolted into your home, or off-site storage like a bank safe-deposit box. There are safes available that hold hanging file folders. That makes it easier to access any paper quickly.

No matter what you choose, you may want to consider keeping copies of your originals in the binder in case of emergency or evacuation. Also confirm that you have a list of the locations of any documents you store in a safe or off-site from your home. If someone else needs to obtain the documents for you, it is vital that you are certain of their location.

I recommend making sure you keep the following documents in a safe:

- *Birth certificates*
- *Social Security cards*
- *Passports*
- *Adoption papers*

- *Death certificates*
- *Marriage licenses*
- *Divorce decrees*
- *Custody paperwork*
- *Appraisal paperwork for jewelry or large purchases*
- *Stock certificates*
- *Retirement paperwork*
- *Mortgage information*
- *Diplomas*
- *Taxes for at least seven years*
- *Power of attorney paperwork (active)*
- *Wills (current, active)*
- *College funds*
- *Trust documents*
- *Business agreements and contracts*
- *Military records*
- *Life insurance (until death or expired)*
- *Medical records*
- *Certificates and licenses*
- *Photos or video of inventory or valuables*

Congratulations! If you have been actively sorting your paper as you read, you too have incorporated the Paper Solution in your life! The number-one question I receive at this stage in paper organizing is, "How do I make sure my paper doesn't get out of control again?!" Maintenance is the answer to that question.

CHAPTER 17

Maintaining Your Systems

How to Stay Organized Even When Life Happens

....

FACT: 1 out of every 10 Americans rent off-site storage—
the fastest-growing segment of the commercial real estate
industry over the past four decades.

(Jon Mooallem, "The Self-Storage Self," *New York Times*, https://www
.nytimes.com/2009/09/06/magazine/06self-storage-t.html?em&_r=0)

....

We all want paper to be done once and for all. However, the
reality is that managing paper is like brushing our teeth, doing
laundry, washing dishes, and buying groceries. It is a constant
part of our lives. More paper comes in every day, and some old
paper is no longer needed. In order to keep our paper organized, we need to commit to regular maintenance.

Each part of our paper system needs to be maintained.
The Sunday Basket gets checked every Sunday. At least three
times a year, the category names on the slash pockets need to
be evaluated and updated. The reference binders need to be

maintained as well. I tend to go through my binders every season and my filing cabinet at tax time each year.

The following is my recommended schedule for binder maintenance. I like to schedule my binder maintenance along with normal seasonal events that either create new paperwork or provide natural reminders to focus on certain areas of our life in paper. It matters little *when* you review and update your binders, but it is vital that you not skip this step. If you used to have a big pile of papers on top of your filing cabinet you had to riffle through when you needed to find something, stacking your new papers on top of your binders will leave you with the same problem.

A major reason I am such a big fan of slash pockets is that it is simple to slide an old bank statement out of a pocket and replace it with the updated one. You do not need a hole punch, you do not need to open and close the binder, and you do not need to commit a significant amount of time to putting your paper away.

Household Reference Binder. This can be updated throughout the year. I typically recommend choosing a time of year when you are OK being inside and working on paperwork for at least one day. A rainy spring day when you want to plan your garden is a good choice. A cloudy fall day is a great time to incorporate any changes you made to your home over the summer. A cold winter day is a great time to review your appliances and schedule the maintenance for the upcoming year.

Financial Organizing Binder. In the US, the most obvious time to update financial information is during the

New Year. Many financial accounts provide year-end statements on or around December 31. Additionally, tax paperwork starts arriving after January 1, and taxes must be filed by April 15 in the US. If you are someone who likes to work in small batches, keep updating your paperwork as it arrives. If you prefer to work in bigger chunks, gather your incoming paperwork in your Sunday Basket and file it in the binders in one big batch.

Medical Organizing Binder. As a mom, the most logical time for me to update my kids' Medical Organizing Binders is right before they go back to school. As we get ready for a new year, we have annual physicals and want to make sure that the school has updated information about the kids' medical history. If you are single or are caregiving for an adult, pick a time that makes sense for their medical needs. You may want to schedule a review around an annual medical exam or a birthday or a date that makes sense to you.

Household Operations Binder. Because the Household Operations Binder has so much holiday and event-planning information, I like to review and update it in the early fall, after the back-to-school crazies are finished but before the winter holiday rush is fully upon us. I also recommend dropping inside a slash pocket any notes you have after an event, like a kid's birthday party or after you finish with holiday decorations.

School Memory Binder. I think the best time to sort school paperwork and file away the keepers is early into summer break. It is fun for the kids and parents to look back over the school year, select the best papers, slip any end-of-year awards into slash pockets, and discard anything you do not want to keep as a long-term memory. Over the years, as the binders get full and papers become less sentimental, it can also be helpful to go back through previous years and get rid of anything that is no longer meaningful.

IEP Binder. The IEP Binder is a dynamic item that needs frequent updating. Honestly, often the reality is that so many things are happening and changing at once that it feels impossible to stop and update your binder. I've been there, and I totally relate. My best recommendation is to keep extra supplies (especially paper and slash pockets) inside the binder and to use any time you have when you are waiting for appointments or meetings to slip papers into pockets where they belong or update any of the printables.

What Happens When Life Happens?

Now, there are some times when organization just seems impossible. So far in this book, I have done my best to provide instruction for all the different kinds of paper. However, life is full of unexpected events that disrupt our best-laid plans. Other times, we are dealing with mental health or physical issues that limit our energy for organizing projects. In the Organize 365 Facebook groups, many of you mentioned being challenged by being chronically ill and needing to feel healthy and energized enough to get out of bed, let alone get working to organize your papers. Others expressed the need for kid-free time in your home, which is something I understand completely. All these are legitimate reasons for not getting your paper organized. So does that mean you are doomed to a dysfunctional household full of unhappy, disorganized people? No!

Unfortunately, I do not have a magic wand that will make it easier to get organized. I have provided several different systems in this book, and I recommend starting with just the Sunday Basket. Keeping your most active, incoming paper organized is critical to the rest of the system working. In the rest of this chapter, I will share some strategies and recommendations I have learned over my years as a professional organizer.

Unexpected Events

Do you have two or more children? Each additional child and stage requires additional adjustment and reorganization of your space and days. One good bout of the flu and our home spirals out of control. It takes a while to get the laundry caught back up and the kitchen clean again. But I can do it, because I have a system that works once I get caught up. The same is true for your paper. In order to feel less overwhelmed, you need systems. Maybe you just want to tackle your paper. Hold on tight, folks—it's about to get emotional! I am going to talk about how to manage items related to your hopes, dreams, and memories that are still in paper limbo.

Organizing During Illness

It is important that you hear me say this: your health is of the utmost importance, and you should prioritize your own well-being above all else. Do what you can (five minutes here, five minutes there), but do not overexert or make yourself ill in the name of organization.

One of the most useful ways I have found to understand chronic illness is Christine Miserandino's Spoon Theory (https://butyoudontlooksick.com). You may have already heard of this, especially if you have or know someone with a chronic illness. This theory outlines the fact that those living with an illness, whether it is visible to the outside world or not, simply have less capacity for activities than those who are not living with an illness.

People with a chronic illness may find it difficult to both wash their hair and cook themselves breakfast. Basic tasks of daily living can deplete all their available energy. For someone in that situation, paper organization can feel like an unachievable dream. Unless the illness goes into remission, they simply may not ever be able to get organized.

If you are truly unable to get out of bed most mornings, you may have already arranged to have someone help you with your daily tasks. You may have a family member, a home health aide, or a housekeeper. If at all possible, you may be able to rearrange the tasks your helpers are completing to help you reach your goal of paper organization.

Asking for help getting organized is not selfish. It is not needy. It should not be just a hope or a wish. As we reviewed in the beginning of the book, having a disorderly, cluttered home actually increases cortisol in the body. You know what impairs healing? Cortisol, stress, overwhelm, and depression. I have said this before and will continue to remind you: it is vital to your health and your quality of life that you do not live in chaos.

Simply put, you need help. At some point in life, we all need help. It is not something to avoid or be ashamed of. Whether it is a professional organizer who comes to your home, a virtual professional organizer (the internet is amazing!), a mother's helper, a housekeeper, or some combination of these, if you need help, get help. Getting your papers organized is important. Your health and well-being are also important. If you are living with a chronic illness, often you simply cannot take care of both on your own. There are many ways to get help, and not all are as costly as you may imagine. At least reach out and explore as many different options as your energy will allow. Be good to yourself, and remember, even the mental practice of listening to the *Organize 365 Podcast* is progress. You can do this.

Organizing with Small Children

When you have young children who constantly need you, you are lucky to get your hair washed on a regular basis, let alone sort your papers. You are stressed to the max and cannot conceive of adding one more thing to your plate. Trying to get organized feels like shoveling snow during a snowstorm. It is a struggle to get any traction or make any progress. The problem is, not having your paper organized leads to even more stress. You cannot organize because you are stressed, but you cannot *not* organize because you are stressed. You *need* a solution.

You can tackle your papers by spending ten to fifteen minutes each day, but we all know it will take *forever* to actually get organized. You really need a bigger chunk of time to make progress. I realized this when I consider how I approach organizing. I also am just a project-oriented person. I would rather spend my entire day on laundry than do one small load a day because I like being released of the mental burden of a project as soon as possible.

So, if you're in this boat with me, because of children being present in your home or otherwise, you may want to think about organizing your paper as a project and chunk it together as much as you can. How can you get that done when you barely have enough time to form a full sentence?

Step #1: Prepare. What you need to do is think, just think, about where the problem areas are in your paper and what really needs your focus and attention. You can think anywhere—while you are driving, while you are changing diapers, while you are playing just one more game of Candy Land. Start scribbling these thoughts on Post-it notes and index cards and tossing them into your Sunday Basket. And start with that full-size laundry basket for your first Sunday Basket. You want to be able to pile all those loose papers from all over the house in one place.

Step #2: Block Off One Day. Now the hard part. You need a day. One full day, kid-free, partner-free, dog-free, responsibility-free. Not four hours, not five minutes here and there—one full, entire day.

1. Before you start pouting and insisting that would be impossible, I want you to consider this scenario. You have a 102-degree fever and the flu and cannot get out of bed. You call in sick to work. What would happen then? How would your family get taken care of if you could not do it? Would your husband stay home? Would you send the kids to your mom's house? Would you go to Care.com and hire an emergency babysitter?

2. Call 'em in. Take that sick day off work. I mean it!

3. Give yourself permission to take that sick day, except you get to be healthy! You *can* use that day and not have to get an MRI to justify it. Broaden your horizons, think outside the box, and stop making excuses for why the childcare buck must always, 100 percent of the time, stop with you. If you are the primary caretaker for your children (or the primary care arranger), I know this can feel totally unrealistic and indulgent, especially if you do not bring in financial income. But no matter what you earn financially, you bring a lot of vital, life-giving aspects to your family, and it is time you stopped letting dollars dictate your value. Even if it is just for one day! If you can spend just *one* day to get your Sunday Basket up and running (and your recycling and shredding out of the house), your active paper will be at least 80 percent organized.

Warning: Progress Leads to New Frustrations

It is important to note that there is no right or wrong when it comes to home organization. Just like there is no perfect weight for a woman or no perfect way to feed a baby, everyone has a different level of home organization that is right for them and makes them happy.

Also, it is quite often the case that the more progress you make in some areas of organization, the more frustrated you get in other areas. This is completely normal, and it just signifies a new level of organization that you expect. You raised the bar, and you now need to stay above that bar or else it gets frustrating.

It is really important to understand that you are in the driver's seat and the change that you require will happen not just *to* you but rather *by* you. You need to make it happen. Do not wait for someone to come rescue you, because believe me, I have been there and that will not happen!

CHAPTER 18

Going Digital(ish)

When to Scan and How to Integrate Digital Solutions to Paper Organization

FACT: The average office has nineteen copies of each document, spends $20 in labor to file each document, spends $120 in labor searching for each misfiled document, loses one out of every twenty documents, and spends twenty-five hours re-creating each lost document.

(PricewaterhouseCoopers, as cited in Sherry Borsheim, "Organizing & Time Management Statistics," *Simply Productive*, March 12, 2012, https://www.simplyproductive.com/2012/03/time-management-statistics)

To be honest, until last year, I didn't take the time to digitize my binders and household records. Raising two kids and meeting all their medical, educational, and physical needs, in addition to starting and growing my business, took every minute I had. It felt redundant. I am the sole organizer and fetcher of paper resources in our home. I can count on one hand the times

Greg, my husband, has needed a paper from me. Being able to grab a binder and go to a meeting met every need I had until Joey went to college.

As my kids are transitioning into adults, and my business has me on the road more and more, I am now finding a need to access my documents digitally. I tell you this because in my opinion, digital is not necessary for most. Digital has added a second place I need my information to be updated and maintained.

At this stage of my life, it is necessary. If anything should happen, I want Joey to have his Medical Organizing Binder on his phone as a PDF if he needs it. Both kids have their current list of medications in their phones as a contact, and both have needed that information in the past year. And that is exactly when and why I suggest you go digital: when you want the ability to access or share your information with other family members and professional service providers who are working with you.

I cannot tell you the peace of mind I have knowing my family has information in our respective binders. We have and use all the basic binders, and each member of my family has a School Memory Binder, as well.

It was not super easy to complete my family binders. It was not as though I took my binder out of the box and immediately got everything squared away. I had to work on it, like I would a jigsaw puzzle, and it took a few months. I also have to set aside time to review the binders and update the contents each year. For me that means I print out digital information or add a note in my binder about where to find that digital information if needed.

In creating your Sunday Basket you have decided for your

household how you are going to merge your digital life with your paper mail and to-do lists. I personally print emails, receive paper bills, and write out my week on paper even though I respond to emails online, pay bills automatically online, and live my daily life from multiple Google Calendars. Everyone's life is a blend of analog and digital. This chapter is a starting place for you to think about what digital solutions will work for you so you can better search out and find a digital expert to help you create your digital solution.

My go-to paper-organizing solution is to maintain my paper binders. I keep the analog paper copy in my home, and I have it to grab when I have medical appointments or if we would have to evacuate our home at some point. At the same time, I do have a backup digital copy in case we lose the physical copy in some tragedy.

It is not super difficult to get the binder digitized. One binder at a time, I took the printable papers with the core information and ran them through my scanner. I then created a PDF document for each binder. I now have the ability to email or text the document to anyone.

Purge, Then Scan

Although we are all waiting for a paperless utopia, the reality is that we must deal with our actual paper before we can begin to digitize. If we scan and save all the paper without decluttering, we will end up with a hard drive full of junk and still be disorganized. We cannot save everything, and really there is no need to try. The first part of purging is the hardest. Once we get used to letting go and living without the piles and files, we will get better at getting rid of what no longer serves us.

Create a Digital Filing System

As you begin your digital storage, I recommend you establish what the digital community calls a "file-naming convention." This means that you make up some rules about how you will name your files, and then use the same information in the same place in the name *each* and *every* time you name a document. Consistency is key in having organized digital files. The most important part of having digital information is to be able to retrieve it when you need to find something. Having simple, accurate file names helps tremendously in being able to find what you need.

One of the most important things you can do is to come up with a system for naming your digital files. You want to be sure you have enough information in your file name to be able to easily sort and retrieve the information you need in the future. As digital searching continues to improve, often your device will search for words in the document itself in addition to the words in the file names. Despite this, it is still easiest to decide on a file-naming convention and to use it consistently. When naming files, you should consider using things like a person's name, a project name, a location, initials, dates, version numbers, and similar data points.

- *Think about how you look for documents. Do you often think about a date first? Or the type of document?*

- Choose file names that are descriptive. The name should give information about the content of the file—who or what is the file about? When was it made? Is it a progressive version of information? Who is the author? The name should help identify the contents without your having to open the document.
- Use a similar order of information each time you name a file.
- When you use numbers, use "0" as a place holder in any blank spots so that items sort in order. For example, if you plan to have up to 999 items that are numbered, use "001" for the first one (i.e., do not use "1," because then "11" will sort next).
- Once you have established your file-naming plan, leave a Post-it note or index card near the place where you scan or create documents to remind you of the way you name files until you develop a good set of habits.
- Similarly, if you are using initials, consider using three letters for that as well (i.e., include middle initials, so for "John F. Kennedy" you would use "JFK" rather than "JK").
- Make a list of the common abbreviations you use for your types of files.
- The name should help you sort for or retrieve the information you need.
- If you post online, names of photos and files can help in your search engine optimization.
- File names help to sort a long list of documents or photographs into similar categories.

- *As you scan down your list of file names, can you easily find what you want as you scroll through? If not, work on your file-name rules.*

Digital files are generally viewed in a list form. They can be listed alphabetically by file name, they can be sorted by size, or they can be sequenced by the date created or last modified. Most programs will sort special characters like a period, asterisk, or exclamation point to the top of the alphabetical list. If you are using a date to start your file name, it is usually best to start with the four-digit year, the two-digit month, then the two-digit day. For example, a scanned copy of an oil change receipt on January 31, 2020, for your Nissan might be named something like:

2020_01_31_OilChange_Nissan

This way of using dates defaults into a simple way to look through a list of documents so that they sort in order of occurrence. If your brain works so that you would look through a list for the car first, and then the date, you could reverse your file name and title it:

Nissan_OilChange_2020_01_31

Alternatively, you can just leave out the space or dividing character and just use capital letters to begin each new word. This would look like:

NissanOilChange20200131

Depending on your device, file names can sometimes accommodate a space, a dash, or another placeholder in place of the underscore. Your file programs will give you information about the kinds of characters that are allowed and forbidden for naming files.

When using version numbers for a document, use at least two digits for the number. This helps the different versions (up to ninety-nine versions) to sort correctly when using alphabetical number. That would mean you would have:

2020AnnualBudgetV01

2020AnnualBudgetV02

For photos, typically you will want to include the following information in a consistent order: date, place or event, photo number for that place or event, person involved, and any special comments. So, 20201225Disney215SallyBreakfastWithMickey would show you that on December 25, 2020, you took your 215th photo at Disney and it was of Sally during her breakfast with Mickey.

When you scan documents using a scanner and a file is saved to the computer, the scanner typically assigns a file name using the convention programmed into the scanning software. Typically, the scan includes the date, time, and sometimes a page or document number. If you scan your mortgage statement first and a birthday card from your grandmother next, the files will have similar names. These files can (and should!) be renamed. Typically, you can just single-click on the file and the name portion becomes editable. Alternatively, on most files, you can right-click and the option to rename the file becomes available. This is an easy way to rename the file.

Now, as you've heard me say a bunch of times in this book,

progress over perfection! Spend some time and make a plan for how *you* will name *your* digital files. Start with the very next file you create, open, or otherwise use. Update the file name for that file. Follow your rules. Start a new folder, and allow yourself to put *only* properly named files inside that folder. You can even gather up all your old documents and folders and put them in one giant file labeled "archives" or "old files" or "clean up" or something similar. Because digital storage is so cheap and easily available, it is unlikely that you will need to find or reference many of those old files. If you do find that you need to access an old file, update it when you find it and move it into your clean storage system. Just like you need a home for each of your physical belongings, your digital files need homes.

On a PC, most downloaded files default to being stored on the left side of the dashboard. One technique I have focused on over the years, as I have gained more and more digital documents, is to rename my files and then drag them to the right side of my computer dashboard. Any files that need to be renamed, filed in a folder, or otherwise dealt with I leave on the left side of the dashboard, and the placement there serves as a reminder to finish my work on the file. If you are inclined, it can be helpful to do an internet search to change the default storage location of your downloaded and newly created files to save things to the right place on the first try.

If you have extra time and want to work on your digital organization, or if you realize that you need to declutter your digital storage, you can work on your backlog of old files with disorganized names. Begin with one file and delete anything you are sure you no longer need. I also recommend deleting anything you can find reasonably easily with a digital search. For example, if you decided to plan a trip to Italy, you would most likely do an internet search and read reviews and different lists of "the best places." It is unlikely you would remember that you had a downloaded copy somewhere in the depths of your hard drive. Clean it up, and get it out. This can be a perfect project to do during a movie night or on a rainy day. Just tackle one small corner of your device at a time and declutter as much as possible.

For more information and recommendations on naming files, you can go to https://library.stanford.edu/research/data-management-services/case-studies/case-study-file-naming.

Find a Decent Scanning System

After all this time, I hope you are not surprised to hear me say that you should not let the quest for the "perfect" scanner slow your progress. As always, progress over perfection, and done is better than perfect. If you really need a copy of something, a low-res digital copy might get you far enough for now. If you lost your home in a fire but have a decent copy of most of your binders, you will be much better off than if you have no information or if all your paper burned up in the filing cabinet because you did not want to write on the printable pages.

Almost every smartphone on the market today takes a decent picture. Get your papers organized, get them at least basically digitized, and back up your electronics. This is the minimum to be safe and to declare the project "done."

When scanning, the higher the resolution, the slower the scan and the bigger the file you need to store. If you are just keeping your oil change receipts for your vehicle (you do know your mechanic or oil change place keeps those records and you can request a printout, right?), make a quick-and-dirty copy. If you are traveling and want to have a copy of your passport, make sure it is good enough to read the numbers and data in case you need to email it to yourself at the embassy. Rarely in life do we need our digital backups. Most of us do not lose our homes to disasters. But get a good enough option in case you do have an emergency.

A super simple way to save papers electronically is to print to PDF whenever possible. When you have a page on the computer or your phone you can print, often one of the options is labeled "print to PDF." Instead of sending the document to the printer, that option will save a copy as a PDF on your device. You can then add it to your digital storage system (email, cloud backup, commercial program, etc.). This can be especially helpful when you need a copy of a document for travel. This option allows you to save the document to the device so you can have access no matter what your data or Wi-Fi connection may be.

If you are committed to doing a large paper backup to a digital system, a scanner with multiple-page capacity is really the best option. As a bonus, those machines can often scan photos as well (which would be a great project once your home and paper are organized).

I have been researching scanners for well over a year, and the scanner I chose is the Fujitsu ScanSnap iX500.

I chose the Fujitsu ScanSnap iX500 for many reasons:

- **It's wireless.** *I don't need any more wired devices in my house! And I wanted the ability to place the scanner anywhere (like in the kitchen) or be able to take it to the basement filing cabinet without having to take the computer with me.*
- **I wanted to be able to scan my backlog of paper quickly.** *The ScanSnap iX500 can scan up to twenty-five pages per minute, and it scans both sides of each sheet. Additionally, blank pages are eliminated as they are scanned, so I can just stack and scan!*
- **I wanted a scanner that would scan to my phone.** *As my business and life become more and more mobile, I wanted to make sure the scanner I was buying would keep up with my ever-on-the-go lifestyle.*
- **I needed the files to be available online.** *I have waited so long to start scanning my documents. As I see technology advancing, I want access to my paper documents from my phone or any other device. I have chosen to use Dropbox as my online filing system. I'll fill you in just as soon as I figure it out!*
- **I wanted a scanner that would read business cards.** *Crazy, I know, but I have saved business cards from the past twenty years of networking and have yet to create a good system for using that information!*

Digital Storage Options

There is a multitude of digital storage options. There are systems like Google Drive, where you get free storage with your free email account. There are "freemium" accounts like Evernote, where the basic plan is free and additional features cost money. Apple has iCloud. Microsoft offers OneNote. Honestly, in today's world, the options, prices, and terms of storage change so quickly that they would be out of date between the time this book gets published and the time it ships to those who preordered it. I do not recommend any one program, product, or website.

However, I will tell you that my team often uses Google Drive. There are people who have security concerns about any company that has access to your email, photos, and documents. I do not necessarily recommend storing copies of your Social Security card and driver's license in an online account with a password that is "password" or "12345." But for many basic items (like a list of paint colors or a meal plan) these services can be an excellent choice.

An alternative to cloud storage for digital files is to do a local backup to a USB drive or an external hard drive and store the hardware off-site (in a bank safe-deposit box or other secure storage site). This is somewhat cumbersome because you end up schlepping a device back and forth. One way to make this easier is to have two external drives, one at home and one at the bank. After you perform your (weekly, monthly, quarterly, yearly) update at home, you would swap out the updated drive at the bank and bring the older, non-updated one back home.

Again, I am a functional organizer, and although I do know some website design, I am not a technology expert. My biggest goal for you is to reduce the papers in your home by 50 to 80 percent and to maintain a system of organization for the rest. I really think that a digital backup is just icing on the cake.

Here are some of the potential digital storage options with a little bit of information about them. Again, I do not recommend any of them in particular, but I recommend you do some research and consider what goals you have for your digital storage.

Backup

At a minimum, you need to have a system and a place to back up your digital files. All hard drives eventually fail. It is not a question of *if* it will fail, but *when*. How many pictures, documents, and files are you willing to lose?

When backing up, let's realize we are all human. We all know we *should* back up, but we want to do a bit more research first, or we need to go buy an extra hard drive, or we need to set up the software. A partial, incomplete backup is far better than no backup at all. A messy backup of a bunch of files you don't actually need is better than not starting your backup at all.

Set aside about an hour on your calendar, and plan to do an internet search for your brand of computer and backup systems. Look for an article within the past year or two that compares a few options. Spend about fifteen minutes looking at two to four of the most commonly described options, and pick one. Order the hard drive. Or sign up for the backup program and start installing the software. Do not delay.

A backup can be as simple as scheduling a recurring backup of your hard drive to an external hard drive. If you often move your laptop, set yourself a phone alarm or reminder to hook up that drive and run the backup program.

If you are looking for an easier way to keep an up-to-date backup, you can enroll in a subscription for an online cloud-based backup. Again, I want you to do your own research. See what parts of your computer storage are backed up. Investigate how you would retrieve your stored files if needed after a hard drive crash. How much data is included at your price? How often is the backup program checked? What is the cost? How many devices in your home are included at that price?

Portable devices like iPads and Android tablets have some backup protection that can be included for free. These back up app downloads and purchases. Many of them also back up photos and contact information. The quality of the backup and the price for exceeding the minimum amount of data varies and changes. Again, be vigilant about how much and what you store.

Online Storage Options

In the rest of the chapter, I will give a brief overview and review of *some* online digital systems. Again, technology changes frequently. Software companies open, merge, discontinue services, and go out of business. Do your own research. Read the terms of service. Pay attention to privacy and security practices. Ask what companies do with your information and files. Stay alert to changes in the laws. You don't have to be perfect about these things, but do take responsibility for keeping your own data safe and secure.

To be fair, I listed the following online storage options in alphabetical order. This is certainly not an exhaustive list, and I'm sure I have missed some that are your favorite.

	PRIMARY COMPANY	SYNC	PHOTOS	FREE OPTION
Amazon Drive Focus: File sharing amazon.com	Amazon	Web Mobile Desktop Can select folders but not files.	Yes, unlimited for Prime Members.	No, 5 GB for Prime Members.
Dropbox Focus: File sharing dropbox.com	Dropbox	Web Mobile Desktop Can select folders or files. Keeps prior versions of documents.	Yes, count toward storage.	Yes, 2GB for individuals.
Evernote Focus: Digital file cabinet & note taking evernote.com	Evernote	Web Mobile Desktop	Yes, count toward upload.	Yes, Basic. Upload 60 MB/month.
Google Drive Focus: File creation and sharing google.com	Google	Web Mobile Desktop Can select folders or files. Maintains prior versions of documents.	Yes, must have a Google account.	Yes, 15GB for individuals. Unlimited photo storage if photos are compressed.

	PRIMARY COMPANY	SYNC	PHOTOS	FREE OPTION
OneDrive Focus: File sharing https:// onedrive.live .com/about /en-us/	Microsoft	Web Mobile Desktop Limited folder choice.	Yes	Yes, 5 GB for individuals.
OneNote Focus: Note taking https:// products .office.com /en-us /onenote /digital-note -taking-app	Microsoft	Web Mobile Desktop	Yes	Yes, free app, but requires a Microsoft account and uses OneDrive storage.

Digital file storage solutions increase and change daily. Many books and resources exist for you to find the perfect solution for you and your family now that you have purged and organized your paper. Paper binders will always be the easiest and quickest way to get all your paper records to the proper service professional or family member to help care for you and your needs, so don't stress out about adding on the "perfect" digital solution.

Conclusion

Our time together has come to an end. Whether you have organized your paper piles or let them sit while you read this book, I hope you now have clarity on the kinds of paper you have and how to get it organized.

When my business first started to offer physical products and online trainings for paper organization, even I did not fully believe I could fill a whole book just teaching you how to organize your paper! (The truth is, after doing this for many years, I have enough stories to fill several books—my editor had to cut me off!) I truly believe this system can change and improve lives, starting with the Sunday Basket. I've seen it happen time and time again, and the stories from my clients never cease to make my heart soar.

I have seen homes transform from having papers in the kitchen, the bedroom, and even the laundry room to having just the four basic binders and a working Sunday Basket (with a few tax files in a drawer in the study). That sort of streamlined existence may still be hard for you to imagine, even after reading this book, but I want to assure you that not only is it a realistic possibility—it's realistic for you and your family.

As you read through the Paper Solution process, you learned that being organized doesn't mean you're perfect all the time.

You will still get overwhelmed. Sometimes you'll still bite off more than you can chew. However, organized people have a way of breaking monumental tasks into bite-size pieces. You now have the step-by-step instructions to start sorting your paper. You know how to create a Sunday Basket and go through it every single week. You now have the tools to progress through a busy period and get back on track, even when life gets a little crazy.

Focus on progress, and give yourself grace. If you remember only one thing, make it this: organization is a skill you can learn. It will not happen overnight, but if you are persistent, you will see improvements. *The Paper Solution* has armed you with all the knowledge you need to eliminate your to-do list, ditch the filing cabinet, and add hours to your week. I can't wait to hear about your paper-organization success!

acknowledgments

In January 2012, I created the Organize 365 company with two goals. The first was to reclaim my home and take back my life. Dramatic, I know, but I was so tired of and exhausted by living in reaction mode day after day. The second was to invest the rest of my life into the study of home organization as my final career. I had no idea what that would look like in the end, but I just knew that the disorder in our homes was the number-one thing holding more women like me back from reaching our highest potential.

The Paper Solution is the culmination of those first seven years in business. I have grown so much as a homeowner, wife, mother, friend, sister, daughter, and professional in that time. The 10,000+ hours I have spent analyzing, reading, organizing, and researching our homes and paper have culminated in this work. I'd like to thank so many of you who have been on this journey with me.

None of this would have been possible without my loving husband, whose response to my quitting my teaching job in December 2011 was to nonchalantly ask me how I was going to make money next. No plan. No road map. He has always let me chase every last dream. Greg has let me put our house and children ahead of all else over and over again, giving me permission to be the wife, mother, and homeowner I have always dreamed of.

To you, my professional organizing clients, our time spent together taught me so much as I helped you puzzle through your piles, laughing, crying, and sighing together. I learned so much. I dreamed about your homes and papers, coming up with new solutions to try the next time we met. Your hospitality, trust, and willingness to learn gave me a burning passion to not only get your homes organized but to figure out how to do the same for other homeowners worldwide.

For you, my Organize 365 virtual audience. Thank you for listening to the *Organize 365 Podcast* and asking thought-provoking questions that I can unpack in future episodes. Thank you for enthusiastically embracing the Sunday Basket concept before there was a box, colored slash pockets, or videos! Thank you for investing in your transformation and the Organize 365 brand so we could keep creating and iterating until we hit on the binder solution.

Thank you to the first Certified Sunday Basket Workshop Organizers. Your faith in the future paper-organization industry is paving the way for homeowners to have a place to turn when life spins out of control and they need to get their papers organized in a hurry.

If this is not your first introduction to me, then you know I am nothing without the amazing Organize 365 team. Pat, Michelle, Emily, Amy, Sue, Vanessa, and Monique, you all have been instrumental in creating *The Paper Solution*. And we will all agree that, Mary, you deserve the most credit for *The Paper Solution* reaching publication. Mary has listened to every podcast and helped create every binder, printable, and workbox in the Organize 365 product catalog. Mary, your attention to detail, ability to assimilate information into an easily digestible form, and unending energy inspire me. Thank you so much for organizing all our paper-organization content in *The Paper Solution* manuscript.

Several years ago I set out to New York by myself with a dream to publish *The Paper Solution*. Farnoosh Torabi, thank you for creating the Book to Brand event, where I met my future book agent,

Lynn Johnston, and book editor, Michelle Howry. Farnoosh, Lynn, and Michelle, without you there would be no *Paper Solution* book.

I'd also like to thank the team at Putnam—Ivan Held, Christine Ball, Sally Kim, Alexis Welby, Ashley McClay, Gaby Mongelli, Meredith Dros, Maija Baldauf, Emily Mlynek, Tiffany Estreicher, Lorie Pagnozzi, Anthony Ramondo, Sanny Chiu, Janice Kurzius, Diane McKiernan, Beth Hicks, Phil Tuttle, Ajax Abernathy, and Joey Woodruff—for all your support as I brought this book to publication.

Additional folks at Penguin Random House who really embraced this book were Alison Rich, Matteo Costa, Stephanie Bowen, Whitney Frick, Erinn Hartman, and Carrie Neill—thank you.

And finally, I want to thank you. Thank you for being open to a new way of looking at paper organization. Thank you for sharing this book with your family and friends. And most important, thank you for taking the time to organize your household papers. Your future self will thank you, too!

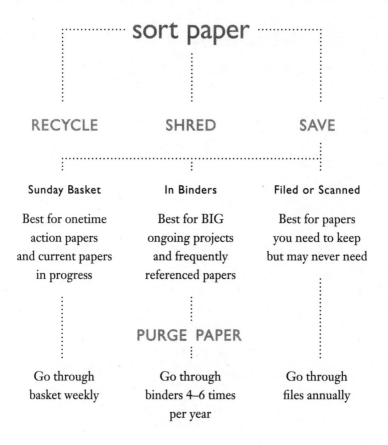

sort paper

RECYCLE	SHRED	SAVE
Sunday Basket	In Binders	Filed or Scanned
Best for onetime action papers and current papers in progress	Best for BIG ongoing projects and frequently referenced papers	Best for papers you need to keep but may never need

PURGE PAPER

Go through basket weekly	Go through binders 4–6 times per year	Go through files annually

to shred
or
not to shred

A quick guide to organizing your financial and household papers

Documents Not to Shred

- Birth and death certificates
- Social Security cards
- Passports
- Pension plan documents
- ID cards
- Marriage licenses
- Divorce decrees
- Business licenses
- Wills, living wills, and powers of attorney
- Military records
- Life insurance policy
- Safe-deposit box inventory
- House deed and mortgage documents
- Annual filed tax returns

Shred When You Get the Next...

- Social Security statement
- Annual insurance policy
- Retirement plan statement
- Investment statement monthly and quarterly

Shred Once You Confirm the Transaction on Your Statement

- Bank deposit slips
- Credit card receipts
- Other receipts unless needed for warranty

Shred When Your Loan, Policy, or Warranty Ends, or You Sell the Item

- Warranty documents and receipts
- Insurance policy
- Loan documents until paid off
- Individual stock purchases

Shred After Seven Years

- Tax return preparation documentation

Shred After One Year

- Pay stubs
- Bank statements
- Credit card statements
- Medical bills—one year after payment or seven years if deducted on your taxes

Shredding Tips

Shredding is $1 a pound at most office supply stores.
A full bankers' box of shredding typically costs around $25.

	monday	tuesday	wednesday
Work Top 3			
Home Top 3			
7 a.m.			
8 a.m.			
9 a.m.			
10 a.m.			
11 a.m.			
12 p.m.			
1 p.m.			
2 p.m.			
3 p.m.			
4 p.m.			
5 p.m.			
6 p.m.			
7 p.m.			
8 p.m.			
9 p.m.			
Dinner			
Chores			

thursday	friday	saturday	sunday

planning time

Weekly Checklist
Work To-Dos

- ☐ Pay bills and get out weekly cash

- ☐ Reboot computer and cell phone

- ☐ Email Inbox Zero (check text and FB messages)

- ☐ Grocery

- ☐ Meal planning

- ☐ Laundry

- ☐ Make an errand list

- ☐ Go through the Sunday Basket

- ☐ Plan my week

- ☐ Place any online orders

- ☐ Dry cleaning and prescriptions

- ☐ Charge Apple watch, tablets, etc.

Weekly Checklist
Work To-Dos

- ☐ _____ _____

- ☐ _____ _____

- ☐ _____ _____

- ☐ _____ _____

- ☐ _____ _____

- ☐ _____ _____

- ☐ _____ _____

- ☐ _____ _____

- ☐ _____ _____

monthly checklist

Home Checklist

☐ Change furnace filter

☐ Change vacuum bag

☐ Check cleaning supplies

☐ Disinfect trash can

☐ Clean microwave

☐ Wash washing machine

☐ Flush garbage disposal

☐ Clean oven

☐ Clean out fridge/freezer

☐ Wash and clean out car

☐ Change bed sheets

Family Management

☐ Check for birthdays/ holidays

☐ 15th reconcile checkbook

☐ Place order for paper products/monthly recurring

☐ Order prescriptions

☐ Check family bathroom supplies

☐ Check monthly lunch account balance

☐ Schedule doctors' appointments

☐ Schedule haircuts

Pets

☐ Flea, tick, and heartworm meds ☐ Wash bowls

Date	Bill	Amount

home improvement tracker

Record the year, project details, contractors involved,
and cost of renovations. Use page protectors to store quotes,
permits, receipts, etc., for each project.

Alarm System

Date	Description

Bathrooms

Date	Description

Drywall/Paneling/Paint

Date	Description

Electrical

Date	Description

ADULT – family information sheet

Name: _____ Date: _____

Maiden Name or Other Names: _____

Address: _____

City: _____ State: _____ Zip: _____

Home Phone: _____ Cell Phone: _____

Birthdate: _____ City/State of Birth: _____

Emergency Contact: _____ Phone: _____

Height: _____ Weight: _____ Social Security #: _____ - _____ - _____

Allergies: _____

Email: _____ 2nd Email: _____

Driver's License #: _____ State: _____

Military/DoD ID: _____

Passport #: _____ Passport location: _____

Spouse's Full Name: _____

Father's Full Name: _____ Birthdate: _____

Mother's Full Name: _____ Birthdate: _____

Employer: _____ Employer Address: _____

_____ Phone: _____

Accountant: _____ Phone: _____

Attorney: _____ Phone: _____

Doctor: _____ Phone: _____

Dentist: _____ Phone: _____

Eye Doctor: _____ Phone: _____

Other Medical Team: _____

Pharmacy: _____ Phone: _____

Preferred Hospital: _____ Phone: _____

High School: _____ Grad Year: _____

College: _____ Grad Year: _____

Other: _____ Completed: _____

health insurance information

☐ Copy of front and back of card

Carrier/Company: _____

Policy #: _____

Group #: _____

Customer Service:_____

Username: _____

Password: _____

☐ Copy of front and back of card

Carrier/Company: _____

Policy #: _____

Group #: _____

Customer Service:_____

Username: _____

Password: _____

☐ Copy of front and back of card

Carrier/Company: _____

Policy #: _____

Group #: _____

Customer Service:_____

Username: _____

Password: _____

☐ Copy of front and back of card

Carrier/Company: _____

Policy #: _____

Group #: _____

Customer Service:_____

Username: _____

Password: _____

ADULT – one-page MEDICAL information sheet

Name: _____

Birthdate: _____ Age: _____ Height: _____ Weight: _____

Address: _____

Emergency Contact: _____ Phone: _____

Backup Emergency Contact: _____ Phone: _____

Caregiver Name: _____ Phone: _____

Primary Doctor Name: _____ Phone: _____

Insurance Information: _____

Preferred Hospital: _____

Dentist: _____ Phone: _____

Dental Insurance Information: _____

....

other important healthcare providers

Name: _____ Phone: _____

Name: _____ Phone: _____

Name: _____ Phone: _____

....

medical problems
- ☐ _____
- ☐ _____
- ☐ _____

medications/treatments
- ☐ _____
- ☐ _____
- ☐ _____

allergies/to avoid
- ☐ _____
- ☐ _____
- ☐ _____

medical equipment
(oxygen, wheelchair, etc.)
- ☐ _____
- ☐ _____
- ☐ _____

immunization record
- ☐ _____
- ☐ _____
- ☐ _____

other important health information
- ☐ _____
- ☐ _____
- ☐ _____

important-dates tracker

January	February	March

April	May	June

important-dates tracker

	July		August		September

	October		November		December

school memory binder

Calendar Year	Age	Grade in School	School Year	Notes

ABC pediatric therapy network

ABC Pediatric Therapy Network
"creating the best life for all children"

Gross Motor Skills	Fine Motor Skills	Speech
By 4 Months	**By 4 Months**	**By 4 Months**
___ Bears weight on forearms when on belly	___ Grasps rattle when placed in hand	___ Sucks from breast or bottle
___ Plays with feet	___ Reaches toward and touches toy	___ Cooing: vowel sounds
___ Holds head in midline	___ Hits at dangling objects with hands	___ Vocalizes some sounds
___ Rolls from back to side	___ Responds to a smile with a smile	___ Produces a variety of facial expressions
___ Brings hands together when lying on back	___ Likes looking at a human face most	
By 6 Months	**By 6 Months**	**By 6 Months**
___ Sits alone for short periods	___ Reaches for a toy when playing on belly	___ Cup drinking is introduced
___ Begins to belly crawl	___ Holds a toy and shakes it	___ Soft, smooth solids
___ Rolls back to belly and belly to back	___ Puts fingers in mouth	___ Moves chewed food to center of mouth before swallowing
___ Grabs feet and brings them to mouth	___ Holds hands open at least half of the time	
___ On belly props up on straight elbows	___ Smiles at self in mirror	
By 9 Months	**By 9 Months**	**By 9 Months**
___ Maintains sitting for at least 60 seconds with hands free to play	___ Waves bye-bye	___ Babbles same sounds
___ Crawls independently	___ Releases objects intentionally	___ Responds to "no"
___ Pulls to stand from floor	___ Feeds self finger foods	___ Vocalizes different syllables
___ Walks with hands held	___ Bangs a toy on the floor	___ Tolerates smooth solid foods
	___ Passes a small object between hands	___ Makes sounds while eating with food in mouth
By 12 Months	**By 12 Months**	**By 12 Months**
___ Cruises along furniture	___ Grasps thick crayon or pencil in fist, does not mark	___ Feeding self with fingers
___ Independent standing	___ Turns pages of a cardboard book	___ Babbles using different sounds
___ Gets into and out of sitting	___ Helps to pull off simple clothing	___ Takes turns vocalizing
___ Corrals a ball with arms and hands in sitting	___ Puts objects into others	___ Points/gestures
___ Transitions sit to stand and stand to sit	___ Pulls shoes off	___ Tolerates coarsely chopped food

notes

Chapter 1. The Paper Tsunami

1. Matt Petronzio, "Average U.S. Office Worker Uses 10,000 Sheets of Paper Per Year," *Mashable*, April 22, 2014, https://mashable.com/2014/04/22/earth-day-paper-infographic.

2. EarthWorks Group, *50 Simple Things Kids Can Do to Save the Earth* (Kansas City, MO: Andrews McMeel, 1990).

3. "Postal Facts: One Day in the Life of the U.S. Postal Service," https://facts.usps.com/one-day.

4. Drew Brucker, "50 Recycling & Trash Statistics that Will Make You Think Twice About Your Trash," Rubicon Global, November 14, 2018, https://www.rubiconglobal.com/blog/statistics-trash-recycling/.

5. "Lost and Found: The Average American Spends 2.5 Days Each Year Looking for Lost Items Collectively Costing U.S. Households $2.7 Billion Annually in Replacement Costs," PR Newswire, May 2, 2017, https://www.prnewswire.com/news-releases/lost-and-found-the-average-american-spends-25-days-each-year-looking-for-lost-items-collectively-costing-us-households-27-billion-annually-in-replacement-costs-300449305.html.

6. Shira Boss, "What Your Stuff Is Costing You," *AARP*, January 3, 2018, https://www.aarp.org/money/budgeting-saving/info-2018/clutter-cost-fd.html.

Chapter 2. The Hidden Cost of Paper

1. Erin El Issa, "Americans Not Paying Bills on Time—and Why That's Bad," *NerdWallet*, August 25, 2016, https://www.nerdwallet.com/blog/finance/paying-bills-time-survey-shows-bad; Kate Ashford, "One in Three Americans Is Late on a Bill," *Forbes*, July 30, 2014, https://www.forbes.com/sites/kateashford/2014/07/30/americans-in-collections/#12c048dc1880.

2. The Ascent Staff, "This Is How Credit Card Companies Hauled in $163 Billion in 2016," *The Ascent*, November 20, 2018, https://www.fool.com/credit-cards/2017/04/13/this-is-how-credit-card-companies-hauled-in-163-bi.aspx.

3. Maureen Campaiola, "How Much Is Your Clutter Costing You?," https://adebtfreestressfreelife.com/cost-of-clutter.

4. Campaiola, "How Much Is Your Clutter Costing You?"

5. Campaiola, "How Much Is Your Clutter Costing You?"

6. Campaiola, "How Much Is Your Clutter Costing You?"; Vanessa McGrady, "5 Reasons Why Clutter Costs You Cash," *Forbes*, January 8, 2015, https://www.forbes.com/sites/vanessamcgrady/2015/01/08/organized-1/#3d59db5951a6.

7. Campaiola, "How Much Is Your Clutter Costing You?"

8. Darby E. Saxbe and Rena Repetti, "No Place Like Home: Home Tours Correlate with Daily Patterns of Mood and Cortisol," *Personality and Social Psychology Bulletin* 36, no. 1 (January 2010): 71–81, http://repettilab.psych.ucla.edu/no%20place%20like%20home.pdf.

Chapter 4. The Paper Solution Program

1. "Organized as You Need to Be," *Times-Standard*, July 30, 2018, https://www.times-standard.com/2013/01/06/organized-as-you-need-to-be/.

Chapter 10. Your Household Reference Binder

1. "Top Five Millennial Real Estate Trends," CRES Insurance Services, August 10, 2016, https://www.cresinsurance.com/top-five-millennial-real-estate-trends.

2. "American Time Use Survey: Charts by Topic: Household Activities," U.S. Bureau of Labor Statistics, December 20, 2016, https://www.bls.gov/tus/charts/household.htm.

Chapter 12. Your Medical Organizing Binder

1. Smitha Gopal, "Health Care Decisions by Generation: How Do Patients Differ?," Rendia, November 6, 2014, https://blog.rendia.com/health-care-decisions-generation-patients-differ. For more generational information, see Sandra Worrell, "Give Millennials What They Need in

Health Care," KevinMD.com, December 6, 2018, https://www.kevinmd
.com/blog/2018/12/give-millennials-what-they-need-in-health-care
.html; Katie Kuehner-Hebert, "Different Generations, Different Health
Care Wish Lists," Benefits Pro, June 13, 2017, https://www.benefitspro
.com/2017/06/13/different-generations-different-health-care-wish-l
/?slreturn=20190028161610; Oliver Wyman, "Complexity and
Opportunity: A Survey of US Health Consumers' Worries and Wants,"
Marsh & McLennan Companies, 2017, https://www.oliverwyman.com
/content/dam/oliver-wyman/v2/campaign-assets/may2017/consumer
-survey/PAR-MKT49701-024ConsumerSurveyreport.pdf.
2. Abby Norman, "'Minor' Errors in Medical Records Can Have Major
Consequences," *HuffPost*, July 3, 2018, https://www.huffingtonpost.com
/entry/opinion-norman-medical-record-errors_us_5b3a534ae4b05127c
ceaf777; Martin A. Makary and Michael Daniel, "Medical Error—The
Third Leading Cause of Death in the US," *BMJ* 353 (May 2016): i2139,
https://www.bmj.com/content/353/bmj.i2139. Published in 2017, the
Pennsylvania Patient Safety Authority found that in 2016, of the
medication errors recorded incorrectly in patient records, 70 percent
were actually administered to the patients they studied: Steve Twedt,
"Medication Errors in Hospitals Don't Disappear with New Technology,"
Pittsburgh Post-Gazette, April 9, 2017, https://www.post-gazette.com
/business/healthcare-business/2017/04/10/medication-error-electronic
-health-record-hospitals-patient-safety-authority/stories/201704090072;
Norman, "'Minor' Errors in Medical Records Can Have Major
Consequences."

Chapter 13. Your Household Operations Binder

1. John Fleming, "Gallup Analysis: Millennials, Marriage, and Family,"
Gallup, May 19, 2016, https://news.gallup.com/poll/191462/gallup
-analysis-millennials-marriage-family.aspx.

Chapter 15. Your IEP Binder

1. "Children and Youth with Disabilities," National Center for
Education Statistics, May 2019, https://nces.ed.gov/programs/coe
/indicator_cgg.asp.
2. "Children and Youth with Disabilities."

3. U.S. Department of Health and Human Services, "Prevalence of Children with Special Health Care Needs," *National Survey of Children with Special Health Care Needs Chartbook 2001* (Rockville, MD: U.S. Department of Health and Human Services, 2004), https://mchb.hrsa.gov/chscn/pages/prevalence.htm.

4. National Survey of Children with Special Health Care Needs, NS-CSHCN 2009/10. Data query from the Child and Adolescent Health Measurement Initiative, Data Resource Center for Child and Adolescent Health website. Retrieved 10/25/12 from www.childhealthdata.org.

index

active papers
  defined, 84
  encountered during the Big Purge,
    65–66
  for the Sunday Basket, 91–92, 120
  vs. reference papers, 53–54, 168
Amazon Drive, 271
Amy (appreciates patients who bring
    their medical records with them),
    204–5
archived papers, storage of,
    242–43
aspiration clutter, 168

Betsy (significant medical records to
    collect), 201–2
the Big Purge
  about, 50–51
  coordination with the Sunday
    Basket, 62
  determining what to purge, 68–69
  emotions encountered during,
    60–61, 62–63, 77–79
  labels, 64
  living with less, 50
  paper-organizing retreat, 59–61
  realistic guidelines, 51
  Recycle box, 67, 80
  Saved Papers box, 65, 71–73, 92
  Shred box, 66–67, 74–75, 80
  supplies, 63–64, 70
  To-Be-Sorted box, 64–65
  Trash box, 67

bills, 123–24
binder system
  active papers *vs.* reference papers,
    53–54, 168
  adding to the, 171
  benefits of the, 176–77
  binder storage, 174–76
  design, 166–67
  digitizing the, 258–59
  financial organizing binder, 54, 169,
    191–200, 248–49
  household operations binder, 54,
    170, 173, 212–21, 249
  household reference binder, 54,
    168–69, 178–90, 248
  Individual Education Program
    (IEP) binder, 170–71,
    230–38, 250
  maintenance, 172, 248–50
  medical organizing binder, 55,
    169–70, 201–11, 249
  optimal specifications, 173
  prioritization, 172–74
  school memory binder, 170, 222–29,
    249–50
  supplements to the, 55, 170–71
  as a way to increase productivity,
    171–72
the brain
  default thinking mode, 135
  depression, 135–40
  retraining, 142
  writing down thoughts to remember
    them, 142

calendar system
  color-coding entries, 153–54
  digital calendars, 148–49, 150–51
  Google Calendar, 96, 97, 102,
    151–54
  to identify time wasters, 147–48
  monthly checklist, 126
  paper calendars, 149–50
  Three New Years cycles,
    117–20, 143–44
cardboard boxes, 242–43
cards and letters, 131–32
challenges
  illness, 252–53
  organizing with small children,
    253–55
  unexpected events, 159–60, 250–51
  while making organization progress,
    256, 273–74
change
  building a habit, 143
  creating physical reminders of ideas
    and goals, 142
  deciding to change, 140–41
  having the right attitude, 141
  maintaining your Sunday Basket,
    143–44
  retraining your brain, 142
  trusting the system, 140–41
Cheryl (overwhelmed by financial
    records), 191–92
Claire (calendar scheduling), 145–47
clutter. *See also* decluttering
  domino effect of stashing, 20–21
  generational considerations,
    32–36, 165
  identifying, 15
  stopping unwanted mail, 76
color-coding
  calendar entries, 153–54
  slash pockets, 93–99, 114–16

containers
  the lure of, 51–52
  vs. functional organization, 57–58
correspondence, 131–32
costs of paper clutter. *See also* financial
    ramifications of paper clutter
  financial, 17–19, 35
  health, 25–26
  mental and emotional, 23–25
  opportunity costs, 27–28
  physical, 20–21
  social, 26–27
  time, 22–23
coupons, 127–28

decluttering. *See also* clutter
  about, 49–51
  aspiration clutter, 168
  digital files, 264–65
  realistic guidelines, 51
  saved papers, 167–68
  setting a limit on school
    papers, 228
default thinking mode, 135
depression, 135–40
digital storage options. *See also*
    technology
  Amazon Drive, 271
  backup systems, 34, 269–70
  Dropbox, 271
  Evernote, 271
  Google Drive, 268, 271
  local backup to an external hard
    drive, 268
  One Drive, 272
  OneNote, 272
  online cloud-based backup, 270–72
disorganization. *See also* organization
  financial costs of, 17–19
  health costs of, 25–26

late bookings and missed
  deadlines, 19
mental and emotional costs of, 23–25
opportunity costs of, 27–28
physical costs of, 20–21
social costs of, 26–27
time costs of, 22–23
dreams and goals
  aspiration clutter, 168
  creating a slash pocket to set
    goals, 142
  making progress on, 27–28
  "someday" concept, 45, 80
Dropbox, 271

Emily (usefulness of a household
  reference binder), 178–79
emotional responses
  during the Big Purge, 60–61, 62–63
  dealing with difficult memories,
    77–79
  negativity, 141
  sentimentality, 77–79, 225, 228
evaluating organization styles
  KonMari system, 37–40
  minimalism, 36–37
Evernote, 271

family members
  ability to access documents
    digitally, 258–59
  color-coding calendar entries,
    153–54
  errand requests by, 101, 109
  family information sheet, 195–96
  and the Sunday Basket, 108–9
file-naming conventions, 260–65
filing cabinets, 8–9, 164–66
financial organizing binder

about, 54
contents, 169, 195–200
creating a household inventory, 197
family information sheet, 195–96
maintenance, 248–49
portability of the, 163–64, 197
setting up your, 194–95, 198–200
settling an estate, 4–5, 54, 169,
  192–93
financial ramifications of paper clutter.
  See also costs of paper clutter
  bank fees and credit card interest,
    17–18
  hidden treasures, 35, 192
  home damage, 21
  late bookings and missed
    deadlines, 19
  medical claims, 14–15
  misplaced receipts, 17
  physical requirements, 20–21
  replacing vital paperwork,
    18–19, 71, 244–46
  unclaimed refunds and gift cards,
    17–18
  wasted money, 18
504 Plan. See Individual Education
  Program (IEP) binder
folders
  slash pockets, 87–88, 93–99, 114–16,
    128, 142
forms, 130–31
Fujitsu ScanSnap iX500 (scanner),
  266–67

generational considerations
  age breakdowns, 32, 165
  Baby Boomers, 33–34, 179–80, 203
  Generation X, 33–34
  going through your parents' papers,
    31–32, 35–36

generational considerations *(cont.)*
  the Greatest Generation, 32–33
  Millennials, 34–35, 36, 179, 213
  "sandwich" generation phenomenon, 213
  the Silent Generation, 32–33, 203
  when moving, 179–80
goals and dreams
  aspiration clutter, 168
  creating a slash pocket to set goals, 142
  making progress on, 27–28
  "someday" concept, 45, 80
Google Calendar, 96, 97, 102, 151–54
Google Drive, 268, 271

habits, developing new, 120–23, 143
health considerations. *See also* mental and emotional costs of paper clutter
  accessibility and fire hazards, 25–26
  depression, 135–40
  dust, 25
  the effect of clutter on mood, 25, 134–36, 139–40
  organization during illness, 252–53
  vermin, 25, 243
Holly (out of control mail), 112–13
home considerations for decluttering
  embarrassment when inviting friends over, 26
  moving to a larger home, 21
  structural damage from clutter and disorganization, 21
household operations binder
  about, 54
  author's experiences with the, 215–16
  contents, 170, 214
  important-dates tracker, 216, 218–19
  maintenance, 249
  setting up your, 220–21
  vacation planning, 173
household reference binder
  about, 54
  author's experiences with the, 180–82, 190
  contents, 168–69, 183–86
  home improvement tracker, 183–84
  maintenance, 248
  manuals, 186
  record-keeping of repairs and renovations, 180–81
  selling your home, 178–80, 182
  setting up your, 186–90

identifying clutter, importance of, 15–16
important-dates tracker, 216, 218–19
Individual Education Program (IEP) binder
  about, 170–71
  author's experiences with the, 230–32
  destigmatizing invisible disabilities, 233
  developmental checklist, 236–37
  maintenance, 250
  physical *vs.* learning challenges, 232–33
  requesting accommodations, 234, 237
  setting up your, 238
  as a way of commanding respect, 235

Jackie (expired passports), 18–19
Jamie (discarding magazines), 46–47
Joseph (active paper management), 81–82

Judy (organized collection of saved papers), 30–32
junk mail, 7, 76

kids' papers, 132. *See also* school memory binder
Kimberly (embarrassment about misplaced items), 26–27
Kim (long-term paper-organizing journey), 241–42
Knill, Holly, 135
Kondo, Marie, 37–40
KonMari system of organization, 37–40

Lauren (benefits of the binder system), 176–77
letters and cards, 131–32
The Life-Changing Magic of Tidying Up (Kondo), 37–40
life stages
  being prepared for unexpected financial responsibilities, 191–93
  effects on paper organization, 11
  going through your parents' papers, 31–32, 35–36
living with less, 50
Liza (household operations binder), 212–13

magazines, 45–47
mail
  junk mail, 7, 76
  opening, 108
  tips for eliminating unwanted mail, 76
maintenance
  frequency, 247–50
  the need for ongoing, 55, 143–44, 172
manuals, 186
Marjorie (misplaced receipts), 17
Mary (household operations binder for the nanny), 217
medical insurance paperwork
  author's experiences with, 13–15, 204
  forms, 130–31
medical organizing binder
  ability to access documents digitally, 258–59
  about, 55
  contents, 169–70
  digital medical records, 201–03, 205–7
  maintenance, 249
  medical information sheet, 205–06
  physical *vs.* learning challenges, 232–33
  saving most medical paperwork, 205–7
  setting up your, 208–11
memories
  emotional responses while sorting papers, 77–79
mental and emotional costs of paper clutter, 23–25, 134–36, 139–40, 252–53. *See also* health considerations
Michelle (serial paper pile shifter), 20
minimalism, 36–37
Miserandino, Christine, 252
monthly checklist, 126

naming conventions for digital files, 260–65
natural disasters and the need for portable papers, 163–64, 197

negativity, removing, 141
neuroscientific considerations
default thinking mode, 135
depression, 135–40
retraining your brain, 142
writing down thoughts to remember
them, 142
notes
adding notes to the Sunday Basket,
93, 116, 120
writing down thoughts to remember
them, 142

One Drive, 272
OneNote, 272
online storage options. *See* digital
storage options
opportunity costs
making room for new opportunities,
27–28
organization. *See also* disorganization
asking for help with, 252–53
author's views on, 52
benefits of, 10, 16–17, 134–36,
139–40
color-coding, 93–99
determining which papers to
keep, 8
file-naming conventions,
260–65
during illness, 252–53
impediments to, 47–48
key concepts, 57–58
as a learned skill, 141
managing household papers, 9–10
minimalism, 36–37

the "paperless office," 6
paper(s)

active papers *vs.* reference papers,
53–54, 168
advantages of, 9
the desire to keep, 36–37
increasing volume of, 6–7
junk mail, 7, 76
storing, 8–9, 165–66
the Paper Solution Program
about, 49–50
diagram, 56
overview, 50–55
perfection, 38, 53, 58
pet care information, 216
photos
sorting and organizing, 40
storage and retrieval, 34
planning
reviewing previous plans, 103
Three New Years cycles,
117–20, 143–44
to-do lists, 103, 106
unexpected events, 159–60, 250–55
for the upcoming week, 102–7,
155–59
your ideal week, 154–55
prioritization
binder assembly, 172–74
schedules and to-do lists, 103–5
Sunday Basket papers,
109–10
progress, making, 27–28, 53, 256,
273–74
projects, 128, 133–34
purchases and returns, 125–27

Rachel (Sunday Basket
structure), 100
receipts
keeping, 124–27
misplaced, 17

Recycle box, 67, 80
Reneé (medical records binder to feel
    in control), 207–8
replacing discarded papers
    concerns about, 16, 69
    important documents, 18–19, 22
resources for eliminating unwanted
    mail, 76
rules
    for determining how to long to keep
        papers, 71–73
    documents to save, 71
    people's love of, 40–41
    for shredding, 74–75
    for using the Sunday Basket, 89–90

safe, using a, 244–46
Saved Papers box, 65, 71–73, 92
scanning documents
    after purging, 259
    author's recommendations, 266–67
    choosing a scanner, 265–66
    file-naming conventions, 260–65
    Fujitsu ScanSnap iX500 (scanner),
        266–67
scheduling
    Google Calendar, 96, 97, 102, 151–54
    monthly checklist, 126
    planning your ideal week, 154–55
    Sunday Basket processing, 102,
        155–59
    task completion, 96
    Three New Years cycles,
        117–20, 143–44
school memory binder. *See also* kids'
        papers
    about, 170
    contents, 225–27
    determining what to keep,
        222–25, 228

looking through your, 224–25
maintenance, 249–50
school tracker for sorting papers,
    226–27
setting up your, 227–29
school papers
    active, 132
    Individual Education Program
        (IEP) binder, 170–71
    school memory binder, 170, 222–29,
        249–50
security considerations
    binder storage, 174–76
    shredding rules, 74–75
sentimentality, 77–79, 225, 228
Shred box, 66–67, 74–75, 80
slash pockets
    benefits of, 87–88, 93–94, 128, 142
    color-coding overview, 94
    additional colors overview, 114–16
    blue, 95–96, 97
    blue (Sunday Basket 2.0 version),
        114–15
    green, 95, 98, 123–24
    green (Sunday Basket 2.0 version),
        114–15
    orange, 94–95, 97
    pink, 114–15
    purple, 114–15
    red, 94, 98
    yellow, 95, 99, 101
social considerations
    embarrassment when inviting
        friends over, 26
    missed events, 26–27
"someday" concept, 45, 80
sorting
    dealing with difficult memories
        while, 77–79
    focusing on usefulness, 42
spoon theory, 252

stashing piles of clutter
   the domino effect, 20–21
   misuse of rooms and spaces, 20–21
storage
   of archived papers, 242–43
   cardboard boxes, 242–43
   digital storage options,
      268–72
   filing cabinets, 8–9, 164–66
   the lure of new containers, 51–52
   misuse of rooms and spaces, 20–21
   physical costs of paper clutter,
      20–21
   in a safe, 244–46
   security considerations for binder
      storage, 174–76
   slash pockets, 87–88, 93–99, 114–16,
      128, 142
   storage units, 8, 19
the Sunday Basket Solution
   active papers encountered during
      the Big Purge, 65–66
   adding Saved Papers to the Sunday
      Basket, 92
   additional boxes, 133–34
   author's experiences with,
      86–90, 96–107, 120
   basket contents, 82–84, 123–34
   basket location, 84
   benefits of, 110–11, 134–36, 139–40
   collecting your active papers, 91–92,
      120
   coordination with the Big Purge, 62
   customizing your system, 114–17
   defined, 52
   FAQs, 107–8
   fictitious example, 85–86
   flexibility of, 113–14, 119–20
   maintaining, 53, 143–44
   making positive progress
      with, 53

   notes added to the Sunday Basket,
      93, 116, 120, 142
   planning for the upcoming week,
      102–7, 155–59
   rules for using, 89–90
   scheduling, 102, 107
   slash pockets, 87–88, 93–99, 114–16,
      128, 142
   trusting the system, 123, 140–41
   as a way to reduce chaos and
      anxiety, 110–11
   weekly routine, 96–99,
      120–22, 143
   and your family, 108–9
supplies for starting the Big Purge,
   63–64, 70

tasks
   prioritizing, 103–5, 109–10
   scheduling time to complete, 96,
      155–59
   task-batching forms, 130
tax paperwork, 242, 243–44
technology. *See also* digital storage
      options
   backup systems, 34
   digital calendars, 148–49, 150–51
   electronic medical records issues,
      205–7
   file-naming conventions, 260–65
   Google Calendar, 96, 97, 102,
      151–54
   home computers, 34
   to increase document retrieval
      ability, 258–59
   online bill paying, 107
   photo storage, 34
   scanning documents, 259, 263
   using a blend of paper and digital
      sources, 258–59

Three New Years cycles, 117–20,
    143–44
tickets, 128–29
time
    late bookings and missed
        deadlines, 19
    operating in "reaction mode," 22
    organizing papers without adequate
        blocks of time, 48
    scheduling time to complete tasks,
        96, 155–59
    Three New Years cycles,
        117–20, 143–44
    wasted searching for things, 8,
        22–23
tips
    for clients with depression,
        137–39
    for dealing with sentimental
        papers, 79
    for eliminating unwanted mail, 76
    for naming files, 260–62
To-Be-Sorted box, 64–65
to-do lists, 103, 106, 131
Trash box, 67
travel, 129–30, 173
trusting the system, 123

unexpected events
    dealing with, 250–51
    illness, 252–53
    planning to allow for, 159–60
    using organizing systems to regain
        control, 251

Victoria (generational uncertainty
    about keeping papers), 35
vital paperwork, 18–19, 71, 244–46

Woodruff, Lisa
    depression, 136–40
    digital calendar system,
        148–49, 150–53
    holiday card supplies, 24
    household operations binder
        experiences, 215–16
    household reference binder
        experiences, 180–82, 190
    increasing need for digital
        documents, 258–59
    Individual Education Program
        (IEP) binder experiences, 230–32
    medical insurance paperwork
        experiences, 13–15, 204
    paper calendar system, 149–50, 152
    paper-organizing retreat, 59–61
    personal experiences with paper
        clutter, 4–5, 10–12
    personal view of organization, 52
    scanner recommendations, 266–67
    scrapbooking consultant
        experiences, 40–41
    Sunday Basket Solution
        experiences, 86–90, 96–107, 120
    tax return organization, 243–44
    Three New Years cycles,
        117–20, 143–44
    travel paperwork storage, 129–30
    as a "warrior," 232

about the author

Lisa Woodruff is a home-organization expert, productivity specialist, and the founder of Organize 365, a multimedia company. Lisa provides motivational and physical resources to help homeowners get their homes organized. Lisa believes organization is not a skill you are born with. It is a skill that is developed over time and changes with each season of life.

Lisa teaches functional, grace-filled organizing through the *Organize 365 Podcast* and is often caught quoting "Done is better than perfect" and "Progress over perfection." Her sensible and doable organizing tasks appeal to multiple generations. Her candor and relatable style make you feel as though she is right there beside you, helping you get organized as you laugh and cry together.

Lisa has been featured in *Fast Company*, *U.S. News & World Report*, *Woman's World*, and *Your Teen*. She has been interviewed on over thirty podcasts and more than fifty local TV segments, and she is a regular *HuffPost* and *ADDitude* magazine contributor.

Lisa lives in Cincinnati, Ohio, with her husband and two children.

You can find more about Lisa at https://organize365.com.